The Good Reverend's Guide to
INFUSED SPIRITS

VOL. IV

Conceived and Created by
**THE REVEREND MICHAEL ALAN
& SONIA KURTZ**

Produced & Obsessed Over by
KELLI HAUGH

Researched & Edited by
CAROLINE MILLS

Photography by
BRE FURLONG & THE QCM TEAM

Creative Direction & Manifestation by
STEVEN GRASSE

Art Direction & Layout by
WADE KELLER & THE QCM TEAM

Cocktail Conjuring by
THE REVEREND & LEE NOBLE

Skyhorse Publishing books may be purchased in bulk at special discounts for sales promotion, corporate gifts, fund-raising, or educational purposes. Special editions can also be created to specifications. For details, contact the Special Sales Department, Skyhorse Publishing, 307 West 36th Street, 11th Floor, New York, NY 10018 or info@skyhorsepublishing.com.

Skyhorse® and Skyhorse Publishing® are registered trademarks of Skyhorse Publishing, Inc.®, a Delaware corporation.

Visit our website at www.skyhorsepublishing.com.

10 9 8 7 6 5 4 3 2 1

Library of Congress Cataloging-in-Publication Data is available on file.
Library of Congress Control Number: 2019943451

Cover design and photography throughout by Quaker City Mercantile

Print ISBN: 978-1-5107-3975-8
eBook ISBN: 978-1-5107-3976-5

Printed in China

The Good Reverend's Guide to

INFUSED SPIRITS

ALCHEMICAL COCKTAILS, HEALING ELIXIRS, AND CLEANSING SOLUTIONS FOR THE HOME AND BAR

VOL. IV

**STEVEN GRASSE PRESENTS: A QUAKER CITY MERCANTILE BOOK
BY THE REVEREND MICHAEL ALAN & SONIA KURTZ**

Skyhorse Publishing

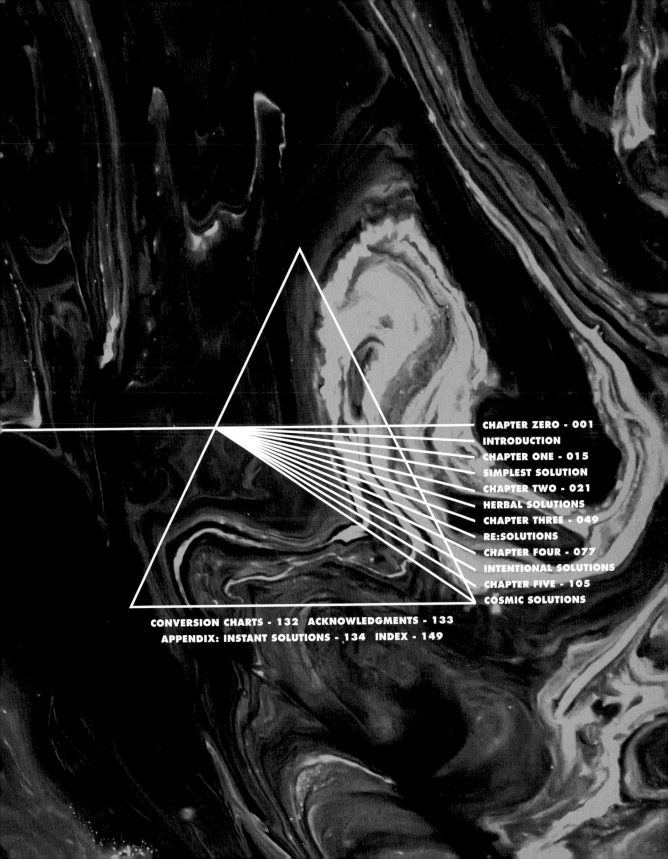

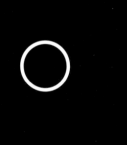

CHAPTER ZERO

INTRODUCTION

"Constantly regard the universe as one living being, having one substance and one soul . . ."
— *Marcus Aurelius*

What is the "Universal Spirit"? The Universal Spirit is a joyous celebration of the limitless possibilities contained within a bottle of great spirits. Indefinitely customizable, it's a DIY kit in a bottle. Add clean water and dilute to make two bottles of versatile neutral spirit, or mix in your own fresh ingredients as the basis for infusions, liqueurs, cordials, tinctures, or household cleaners. Both a look back at the historic inventiveness of our distilling forefathers and a nod to the endlessly changing future, The Good Reverend's Universal Spirit is the perfect solution for the here and now.

While many products similar to those in this book can be purchased commercially, most are merely utilitarian — spirits without any **spirit**. Creating your own infusions with thought and care allows for the true nature and power of the ingredients to shine through.

In addition to these metaphysical benefits, making your own infusions, bitters, tinctures, and other concoctions at home allows you to save money and produce better flavor. Because you maintain total control over the process, you can ensure your ingredients are whole, natural, and of good quality, and tailor those ingredients to suit your palate.

There are satisfying rewards found in taking the corporatized process back into your home and hands. You can create your own "house" spirit, label, and brand. In essence, performing this process is a homecoming; you are bringing to your home a ritual that was originally performed there. You yourself become the creator of something personal, thoughtful, and memorable.

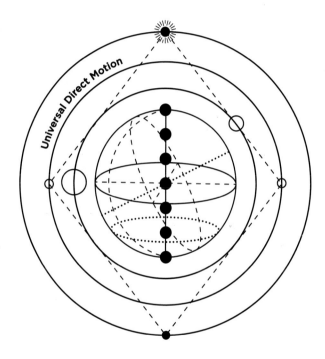

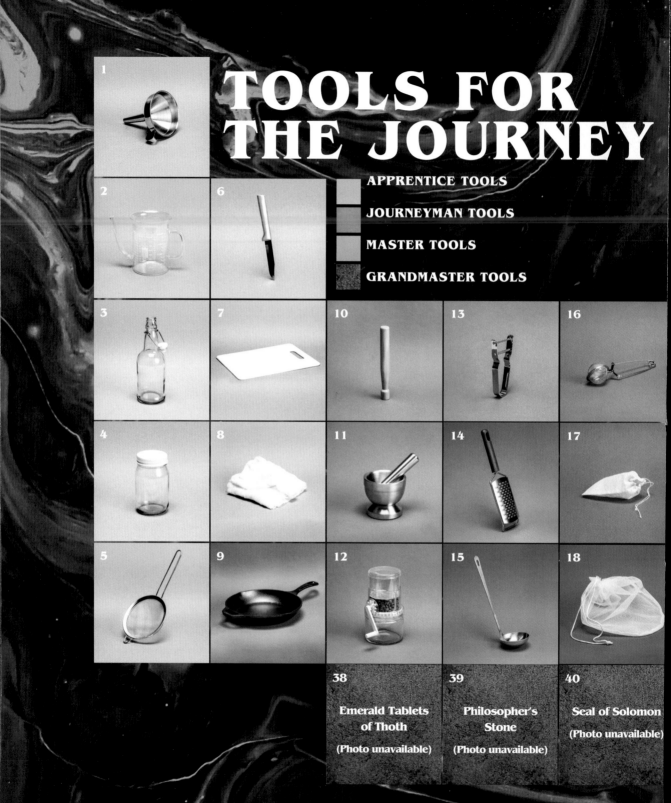

TOOLS FOR THE JOURNEY

APPRENTICE TOOLS

JOURNEYMAN TOOLS

MASTER TOOLS

GRANDMASTER TOOLS

38
Emerald Tablets
of Thoth
(Photo unavailable)

39
Philosopher's
Stone
(Photo unavailable)

40
Seal of Solomon
(Photo unavailable)

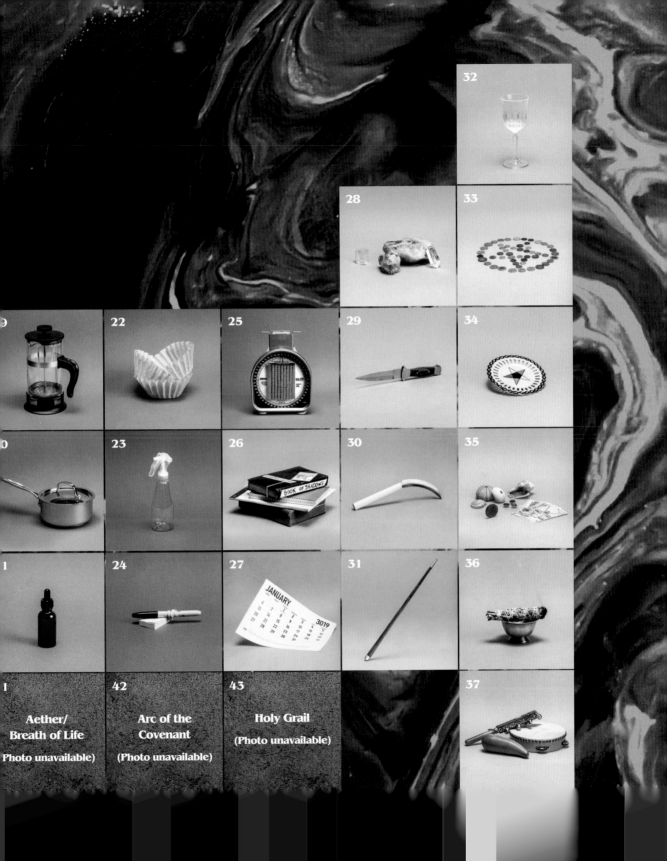

32

28

33

9

22

25

29

34

0

23

26

30

35

1

24

27

31

36

1

Aether/
Breath of Life

(Photo unavailable)

42

Arc of the
Covenant

(Photo unavailable)

43

Holy Grail

(Photo unavailable)

37

EQUIPMENT

IN ORDER TO BEGIN YOUR JOURNEY INTO THE WORLD OF SPIRITUOUS SOLUTIONS, YOU WILL NEED A FEW TOOLS.

APPRENTICE TOOLS

Basic infusions and concoctions only require a few simple pieces of equipment.

1................................Knife
2...................Cutting board
3................Measuring Cups
4..........Infusing containers *
(16, 24, and/or 32 oz, depending on recipe)
5.............Fine mesh strainer
6.........................Cheesecloth/
Clean tea towel
7...............................Funnel
8..............................Bottles
(8 oz or smaller for bitters and tinctures, 24 oz or 750 ml for larger infusions)

JOURNEYMAN TOOLS

9.....................Kitchen scale
10.........................Saucepan
11.................Cast iron skillet
or sauté pan
12..........................Muddler
13.............Mortar & pestle
14...............Coffee Grinder
15...........Vegetable Peeler
16........................Microplane
17.................................Ladle
18...................Steeping bags
19..........................Tea balls
20..................Nut milk bags
21.................French press
22.................Coffee filters
23...............Dropper bottles
24..................Spray bottles
25...................Labeling tools

MASTER TOOLS

26..................Journal/Book of
Shadows
27.............Calendar/Almanac
28...............................Crystals
29................................Athamé
(black handled knife)
30................................Boline
(white handled knife)
31..................................Wand
32............................Pentacle
33...............................Chalice
34.........Incense and censer
35.................Smudge sticks
36..............................Charms
37...............................Totems

GRANDMASTER TOOLS

38...............Emerald Tablets
of Thoth
39..................Philosopher's
Stone
40.........Seal of Solomon
41................Aether/Breath
of Life
42....................Ark of the
Covenant
43...........................Holy Grail

A NOTE ON CONTAINERS
Certain containers work better than others for infusing. Alcohol can leach chemicals or lingering flavors from plastic, so glass jars are preferable. Mason jars with wide mouth openings are readily available, inexpensive, easy to clean and sanitize, and have airtight lids — all important qualities for a successful infusion.

CHOOSING & PREPARING INGREDIENTS

AN INFUSION IS ONLY AS GOOD AS THE INGREDIENTS YOU USE

As alcohol extracts flavor from your fruit, herbs, and spices, imperfections and off flavors can be magnified and produce an impure and unpleasant result. Every element matters — age, freshness, ripeness, manner of growth, and harvest time and location all factor into your final product.

FRESH PRODUCE

For fruits and vegetables, be sure that you are using unwaxed, organic produce — dirt, pesticides or wax on the skin of the fruit is undesirable. Organic ingredients are preferred, when possible. Be particularly mindful with citrus, a commonly called for ingredient in this book, as the outer layer of zest contains all of the fruit's essential oils. In addition, always wash your produce thoroughly with cool water prior to using it in an infusion.

Items that are in season and grown locally are ideal, as they contain more flavor than produce farmed long ago and far away which has spent days, weeks, or even months in transit. Farmers' markets can be a Shangri-la for these types of ingredients, especially unique, unusual, or delicate fruits and vegetables. Since these items are picked within days of coming to market, they also contain more prana (life

> *A NOTE ON NEUTRAL SPIRITS*
> *While all of the recipes in this book use The Reverend's Universal Spirit, other neutral spirits may easily be substituted. The higher the proof, the more intense the infusion, so high proof spirits like Everclear (matching RUS at 150 proof) are ideal. A higher proof (84°-90°+) or even standard 80 proof vodka will suffice. However, keep in mind that infusing at lower strength may require more time.*

energy) than anything found at a supermarket or big box store.

FROZEN PRODUCE

Fresh, local produce is ideal, but for hard-to-find or out of season items, quality frozen fruit is an option. Harvested at peak ripeness and then flash-frozen, frozen produce can sometimes contain even more flavor than its fresh counterparts. Typically, frozen foods don't require washing, but read packaging thoroughly and note any expiration dates.

Some produce loses its shape or becomes mushy when defrosted. This is because the cells that make up produce contain water — and as declared by the laws of the universe, water expands in volume when it is frozen. As the water in the cells expands to form ice crystals, it ruptures cellular walls, leaving the cellular structure unable to hold together upon defrosting.

However, this also means that more juices and flavor are released into your infusion — keep this in mind when diluting, and determining proof (see p 13) for more information on proofing). When using frozen, defrosted fruit simply reduce the amount of water called for in the recipe by a quarter.

HERBS, TEAS, and FLOWERS

Herbs make for glorious infusions and tinctures, desirable not only for their flavor but for their many health benefits.

Since fresh herbs have a short shelf life, it is recommended to use them the day they are purchased — or, even better, the day they are picked. Choose verdant herbs with rigid, firm stems, healthy leaves, and fresh, strong aromas.

As with produce, both fresh and dried herbs can work in infusions. Freshness is important here as well — select dried herbs that have retained color and aroma, and use within 6 to 8 weeks of purchase. Care must also be taken when determining measurements — as a rule, use half the amount of dried herbs that you would if using fresh herbs.

Teas should be selected like dried herbs, and used within the same amount of time. Bulk tea is generally preferable to tea bags, though either will work. When selecting bulk tea, look for crisp, dry, fragrant tea leaves.

Edible flowers such as violets, chamomile, and roses make for excellent ingredients as well. It is imperative that flowers used in any solution have been grown specifically to be food safe. Supermarket roses are treated with dyes and pesticides and should never be consumed.

SPICES, NUTS, and COFFEE

Like herbs, spices are desirable in solutions for their incredible flavor and health benefits.

When possible, use whole spices rather than ones that are pre-ground or powdered, and grind them yourself prior to infusing. This allows for fresher flavor as well as control over the size of the grind.

Depending upon the tools you have at your disposal and the spice in question, there are several options for grinding: a coffee grinder (manual or electric) or small food processor is quick and simple, while a mortar and pestle or other manual method (knife, hammer, rolling pin) are preferred when you're looking for a precisely sized grind.

For whole seeds and dried berries, toasting them in a dry pan on the stovetop immediately before grinding them can bring out more flavor and aroma in the final product. To toast ingredients, simply combine in a heavy dry skillet over low-moderate heat, stirring constantly, until fragrant and a shade darker. Whole spices need only 1 to 2 minutes to release their oils and fragrance, while nuts take closer to 2 to 3 minutes. Ingredients with a larger surface area require longer roasting times: nuts will take longer than seeds, so don't place them all in the pan together.

Nuts contain the energy and genetic information to grow trees, making them an excellent choice for powerful solutions. If purchasing nuts in the shell, make sure the shells are unblemished, with no cracks or rancid odors. Shelled nuts should be firm and fresh. Whole, raw nuts are ideal, though unsalted, roasted nuts will work in a pinch. Unused raw nuts should be stored in the freezer, where they will remain fresh for 6 months to a year (depending on the variety).

Of the many coffee bean options available, it is best to buy roasted whole beans and grind them prior to use. Coffee beans should be kept in an airtight container at room temperature if being used within a short period of time. For longer periods, beans can be stored in an airtight container in the freezer.

SWEETENERS

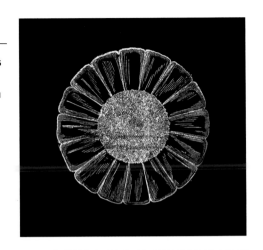

One of the most ingenious features of making solutions from scratch is the ability to control the type and amount of sweetener used. Most recipes in this book are at a moderate level of sweetness — this allows for an increase or decrease to fit personal taste.

Standard, granulated, white sugar is a good place to start when learning how to master solutions. White sugar is easily accessible, inexpensive, and neutral in flavor, which will allow the taste of the infused ingredients to shine forth.

As one gains experience, it is worthwhile to investigate alternative sweeteners to add depth and dimension to the flavor of the solutions.

White Sugar: refined and most flavor neutral.

Raw Sugar: unrefined white sugar. Still very neutral in flavor, the brown tinge is caused by the presence of molasses.

Brown Sugar: White sugar that has molasses added back in. Its caramel-like flavor pairs well with fruit and spices.

Demerara Sugar: Partially refined sugar with large, coarse grains and a pale amber color. Has a natural caramel or toffee-like flavor.

Turbinado Sugar: Similar to demerara sugar, turbinado is less processed than common white or brown sugars. Comes from the first pressing of sugarcane, and retains some of the natural molasses flavor.

Molasses: A byproduct of boiling down sugarcane to the point of crystallization. Very robust, bittersweet flavor; rich in minerals.

Corn Syrup: A form of refined sugar extracted from corn, with a light sweetness.

Agave: A sweetener produced from several species of agave plants, by heating and concentrating the juice or aguamiel to a thick syrup. Sweeter than sugar, light agave syrup has a relatively neutral flavor while darker varieties have caramel notes.

Golden Syrup: Also called "light treacle," common in the UK. Has a light caramel flavor, and is a popular substitute for high-fructose corn syrup or honey.

Honey: About the same level of sweetness as granulated sugar, but with varying flavor and complexity based on floral source, color, and origin.

Maple Syrup: Another natural syrup, created by boiling sap from maple trees until the thick, sweet syrup remains. Comes in two grades, A and B, as well as Light, Medium, and Dark Amber classifications. Has a unique "maple" flavor and silky texture.

Palm Sugars: Made from the sap of a variety of palm trees, including date palms, sugar palm, and coconut palm.

Stevia: Derived from the leaves of the Stevia plant, which contains compounds 30 to 150 times the sweetness of sugar. The body does not metabolize these compounds, and so Stevia contains 0 calories.

Date Sugar: A sweetener made from dates, with butterscotch notes. Can be swapped one-to-one for white or brown sugar, though it does not melt in the same way as processed, granulated sugar.

Monk Fruit: Similar to Stevia, monk fruit sweeteners are made from an extract of the gourd-like fruit which is 150 to 200 times sweeter than sugar and contains 0 calories.

Lucuma: *A Peruvian fruit often found in the US as a powdered supplement. It has a light sweetness with flavor similar to a sweet potato, and contains an array of nutrients, fiber, and antioxidants in addition to a low glycemic index.*

Brown Rice Syrup: *A sweetener made up of glucose, rather than fructose, making it easily digestible — glucose can be metabolized by all of the body's cells. Has an extremely high glycemic index, which causes blood sugar to spike rapidly.*

Barley Malt Syrup: *An unrefined sweetener derived from malted barley. Half as sweet as white sugar, with a distinctive "malty" flavor and dark brown color.*

WATER

Older than our Sun and just as vital to all life on Earth, water is an essential element when creating infused spirits.

To make flavor extraction stronger and faster, the Universal Spirit is distilled at a high proof and it is necessary to add water to make it safe and palatable to consume.

Just as it is important to procure fruits, herbs, and spices from a good source, paying attention to where one sources and how one prepares their water will have a profound effect on a finished tincture, liqueur, or cocktail.

Water should always be clean; distilled or spring water are optimal selections. These waters are the most neutral in taste and will allow the flavors of the infused ingredients to shine through.

If using tap water, running it through a filtration pitcher is a very good idea.

As we are expanding to higher levels of consciousness, it is becoming apparent that water has memory and can be programmed, and these programs can be absorbed into the body when ingested.

No matter the source of water, this amazing aspect of it is a great way to supercharge infused spirits with great energy.

Programming, or structuring, water is easy to do and takes no more than water, a container, and focused intention. Simply fill a clean container with water and think positively about it.

Labeling the container with words like "Love," "Peace," "Joy," or an image of the flower of life is an excellent method to saturate water with those attributes. Adding a couple crystals to the container will also help.

Exposing the container to Solfeggio frequencies or prayers is an also excellent way to program water.

Program the water for as long or as short as possible. The length of time the water is programmed is not as important as the actual action of programming the water.

PREPARATION & MEASURING

INGREDIENT PREPARATION

All produce must be washed thoroughly, and it is ideal to use room temperature, holy water for this. If holy water can not be obtained, a simple blessing over the sink, plumbing, and faucet will do.

Remove any dirt, pesticides, or wax on the skin of the fruit or vegetable and cut off any bruised areas. If using organic ingredients, it is unnecessary to peel items such as apples, pears, or peaches. If not using organic it is recommended that these items are peeled.

Unless noted otherwise in the recipe, ingredients should be broken or ground down prior to measuring. Processing the ingredients in this manner increases their surface area. The more surface area The Universal Spirit can connect with, the more flavor can be extracted into the solution.

Firm fleshed fruit like apples, pears, peaches should be diced into ½-inch cubes before measuring.

Delicate fruit like berries can be slightly mashed or muddled before measuring.

Fresh herbs should be roughly chopped; dried herbs and teas do not require any additional processing.

Whole spices and nuts should be coarsely ground before measuring.

SPACE PREPARATION

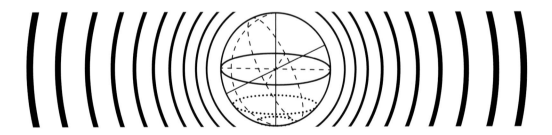

It is always best to work all ways in clean, organized physical and metaphysical space. Taking a couple minutes to consider, cleanse, and focus on the space in which one works will have a profound effect on the result of a project. This is the foundation upon which the work will be built—do not overlook it.

When working at home, select an area that is well lit and simply feels good.

If one feels adventurous, do not limit the work to indoors. Expand outside to a favorite place in the yard or deep in the forest. The better one feels about where they are working, the better the work that will be produced.

If working on a project for a specific event, it is a good idea to have a picture of the venue on hand, or even better complete the work at the venue.

Similarly, if working on a project for a specific person, having a picture of the person nearby is recommended. Consider completing the work in a cherished location that is relevant to the recipient.

Once an appropriate location has been secured, clear the area of any clutter, wipe down surfaces (preferably with a cleaning solution found in chapter 4), clean and lay out all necessary tools for the project.

Burning incense or sage is an excellent way to spiritually cleanse an area. The smoke will push out negative energy while carrying good intentions up to the heavens. Be sure to have a window or door open to give unwanted energy a way to exit.

Alternatively, purposeful loud clapping can also dispel any lingering negative energy in a space. Bells, chimes, gongs, tambourines and/or maracas are also very effective at removing bad juju.

TIME PREPARATION

Time and Space go hand in hand. In considering where one works it is also important to consider when one works.

Humans are mostly made up of water. Just as the phase of the moon affects the tides, it can also affect our spiritual and physical bodies.

The new moon represents a new beginning. The moon is blank, the mind is blank, there is space to be filled. These are choice times to begin work.

As the moon grows, it can play a powerful role in influencing the growth and success of a project.

The full moon represents completion. The moon is full, the mind is full, it is time to complete work and harvest the seeds that were sown on the new moon.

As the moon fades back into nothing, it is time to review the previous cycle, enjoy the what has been harvested and plan for the next new moon.

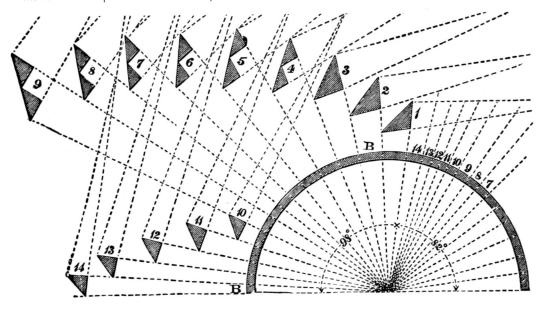

New Moon:
- Start a vacation
- Find good deals
- Start a business
- Attend an interview
- Plant above ground annuals or crops that produce seeds outside of fruit
- Set intentions
- Have surgery

Full Moon:
- Impulse shop
- Conceive a child
- Sign contracts
- Plant bulbs
- Plant perennials
- Transplant crops

Waning Moon:
- Problems in travel
- End a relationship
- Start a diet for weight loss
- Quit a bad habit
- Take out the trash
- Cut/ remove unwanted hair
- Mow lawn
- Slaughter livestock
- Harvest crops
- Cultivate seeds

Waxing Moon:
- Host a party
- Get married
- Go on a date
- Cut hair to promote growth
- Plant annuals, above ground crops that produce seeds inside fruit

The heavenly bodies closest to earth (and that can be seen with the naked eye) have been the subject of reflection and introspection for millennia. These seven classical "planets" are the Sun, the Moon, Mercury, Mars, Jupiter, Venus, and Saturn also known as the Chaldean Order.

Each day, hour by hour, these planets cycle through the sky and influence the Earth with their planetary attributes. These planetary attributes correlate to qualities exemplified by the gods and deities who were originally associated with each planet.

WIth planning, one can harness these attributes and encode them into one's work. Select the attributes that will produce desirable outcomes and determine what planet represents those attributes.

Since planetary hours change daily, and are affected by the time of the year and one's location on Earth, the easiest way to determine when a specific planet will rule the Earth is to consult an online planetary hour calculator or analog chart.

Once the time has been determined, plan your work to this schedule and supercharge the solution.

Planetary Attributes

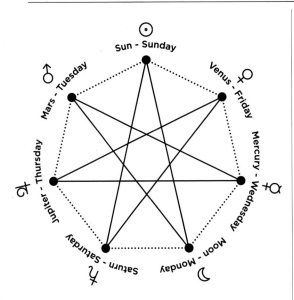

☉ **Sun**
Sunday – career success, promotion, courage, improved health, increase social status

☽ **Moon**
Monday – domestic success, increase imagination, clairvoyance

♂ **Mercury**
Tuesday – courage, mental alertness, physical strength, victory

☿ **Mars**
Wednesday – good luck, improved communication, self-improvement

♃ **Jupiter**
Thursday – success, prosperity, wealth, treasure

♀ **Venus**
Friday – improving relationships, increased beauty, reconciliation, peace

♄ **Saturn**
Saturday – organization, breaking bad habits, self-discipline

MEASURING

For the recipes in this book, fruit should be chopped first and then measured. Note that all measurements in these recipes are listed by volume, not by weight.

DETERMINING PROOF
Since no two apples are the same, the amount of liquid extracted from an ingredient while soaking in Universal Spirit will vary on an infinite amount of elements.

Therefore it is important to understand what proof is and how it is calculated. For example, watermelon will add more liquid to an infusion than an apple.

After straining an infusion, measure the amount of liquid there is. Subtract the amount of Universal Spirit that was used at the beginning of the project to determine how much liquid was extracted from the ingredients.

Once this value is determined, the amount of water (or other dilution liquid) can be adjusted to accommodate for this extra liquid, ensuring the solution is at the proper proof.

> ## RUS = 151 Proof = 75.5% Alcohol
> ## 1:1 RUS:Water = 75.5 Proof = 37.75% Alcohol

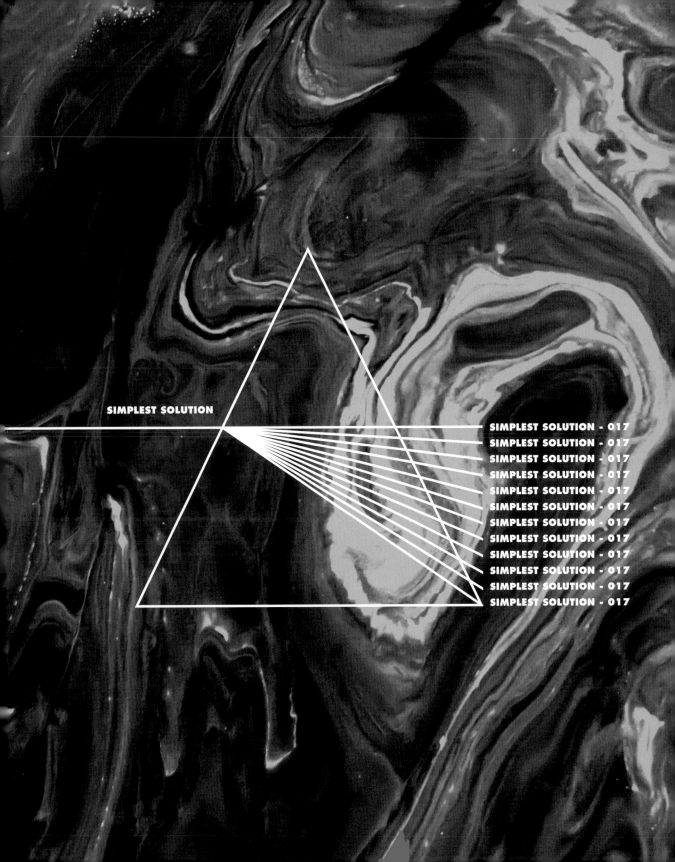

CHAPTER ONE

THE SIMPLEST SOLUTION

THE SIMPLEST SOLUTION IS just that – simple. A 1:1:1 combination of Universal Spirit, fruit, and sugar, the simplest solution is a great beginner recipe for those just commencing their journey into the world of infusions. While any fruit can be used for this infusion, our favorite is an apple. Flavor can change drastically depending on the season and variety, so choose your favorite variety (or mix a few) and chop into ½-inch pieces before adding to the infusion.

INGREDIENTS	INSTRUCTIONS
12 oz Universal Spirit *12 oz chopped fruit* *12 oz simple syrup (p 25)* **"Everything should be made as simple as possible, but no simpler."** — *Albert Einstein*	Combine ingredients in a mason jar and infuse for 3 to 5 days in a cool, dark place such as a refrigerator or cabinet depending on your local climate. After the mixture has finished infusing, strain through a sieve or cheesecloth and discard the excess fruit. Properly stored in an airtight container away from sunlight, the mixture will store indefinitely. *Simple syrup is an easy ingredient to make, requiring only water and sugar. Simply combine a 1:1 ratio in a medium saucepan and bring to a boil, stirring until sugar has dissolved. For the simplest solution, use 1 cup water and 1 cup sugar, which yields 1½ cups (12 ounces). Allow to cool before using or storing. You can keep this syrup in an airtight container for up to 3 weeks.

Fig. 1

Fig. 2

Fig. 3

Fig. 4

HERBAL SOLUTIONS

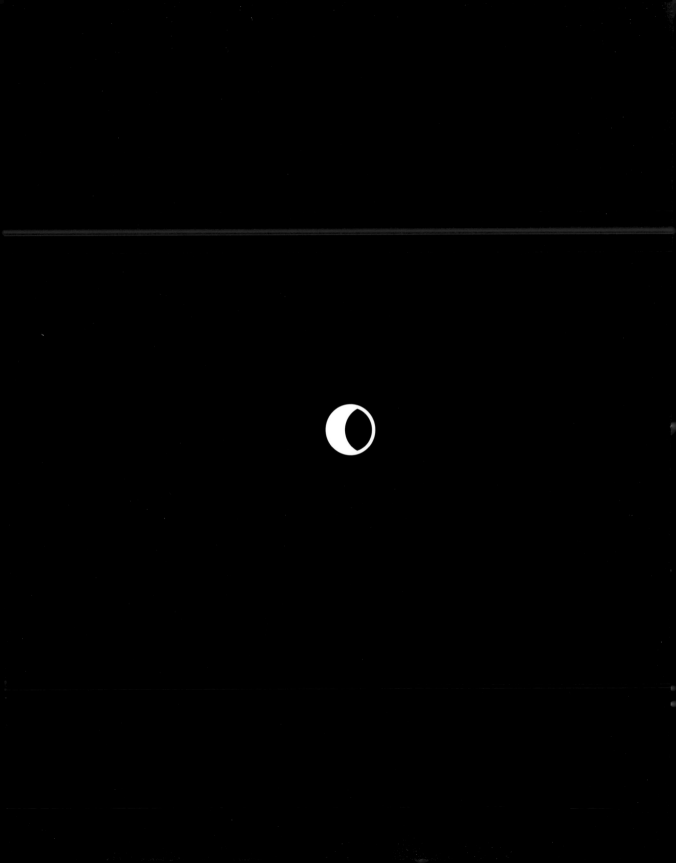

CHAPTER TWO

HERBAL SOLUTIONS

**"In the nice bee, what sense so subtly true /
From pois'nous herbs extracts the healing dew?"**

— *Alexander Pope*

*Nowhere is the power
of the Universal
Spirit more evident
than in the creation
of herbal tinctures.*

High-proof alcohol can extract not only flavor, but magical (and functional) compounds from any herb, spice, or flower, resulting in a powerfully concentrated liquid essence. It also preserves these vital compounds much longer than other methods—tinctures remain shelf stable for several years.

Unlike essential oils, which can be toxic to consume and can be irritating when applied directly to skin, tinctures can be added to hot water or honey to drink, or dropped directly onto the tongue. In addition to their holistic uses, tinctures can be used as incredible drink modifiers — add a couple of dashes into your favorite cocktail, beer, or club soda, as you would use bitters.

Tinctures are available for purchase at a variety of specialty and health food stores, but making them at home offers several benefits, not least of which is decreased cost.

In this chapter, we'll utilize the Folk Method of tincturing. This method is based on ratios — generally 1 part herbs to 2 parts Universal Spirit (or 1:3 if using dried herbs). The strength of the tincture may vary from batch to batch, but this is a result of the more natural method. Trust your intuition and The Universal Spirit to work as nature intended.

ROSE

Rosa rosa

THE ROSE IS A flowering plant grown across the world, renowned for its beauty and fragrance. Roses also hold symbolic meaning in many cultures — in religion as a symbol of the goddess Venus and later the Virgin Mary, in politics as the national flower of England and the symbol of Britain's Labour party, and across art, architecture, and literature more broadly. Apart from their ornamental use, roses are cultivated as an ingredient in perfume, food, drink, and medicine. Rose water is a common ingredient in Middle Eastern cuisine, as are rose syrup and tea made with the flower's buds and petals. Rose hips, the fruit of the plant, are extremely high in vitamin C, and can be made into jams and jellies, syrups, or tea.

Roses are regarded by the holistic community to be both anti-inflammatory and anti-parasitic. In addition, they're known for their ability to lower cholesterol and treat wounds. Add a drop or two of your tincture to your favorite tea to ward off sore throats or combine with body oils such as coconut or jojoba to soothe body cramps and spasms.

ROSE TINCTURE

8 oz Universal Spirit
½ cup fresh rose petals, gently
*   crushed (¼ cup dried rose)*
8 oz water

Steep Universal Spirit and rose petals in an airtight container for 5 to 7 days. Taste test before straining and pressing solids to extract as much liquid as possible. After straining, dilute with water then bottle and store in a cool, dark place.

ROSE LIQUEUR

8 oz rose tincture
24 oz water, divided
1 cup sugar

In a small saucepan, combine 8 ounces of the water over medium heat with the sugar just until the sugar dissolves. Remove from the heat and let cool. Blend the rose tincture, sugar solution, and remaining water. Bottle and seal in an airtight container – ready immediately!

ROSE BITTERS

4 oz rose tincture
4 oz bitters base*
8 oz water

Combine the rose tincture with the bitters base in a clean jar, then dilute with 8 ounces water.

*BITTERS BASE

8 oz Universal Spirit
1 tbsp dried gentian root
1 tbsp dried wild cherry bark
1 tbsp dried quassia
1½ tbsp dried wormwood

In a 1-pint jar with a tight-fitting lid, combine all the ingredients. Be sure all the dry ingredients are submerged in the alcohol. Seal the jar and store in a cool, dark place for 5 to 7 days, shaking the jar daily. Strain the solution into a clean 1-pint jar, discarding the solids. Seal the jar and store at room temperature until ready to use.

SAGE

Salvia officinalis

LIKE MANY CULINARY HERBS, sage is a member of the mint family and native to the Mediterranean region. Its distinctive gray-green leaves have long been integral to English, Italian, and American cuisine.

Sage is often cited as one of four "essential herbs" in British cuisine alongside parsley, rosemary, and thyme.

The species name, *officinalis*, comes from its long history as a healing herb — the word's origin refers to the room in a monastery where medicine was stored. It has been used as a cure for snakebites and wasp stings, a diuretic, an anesthetic, and even to ward off evil and the plague. Sage has also been shown to effectively kill streptococcus mutans bacteria as well as candida albicans, both notorious for causing cavities. Try mixing your sage tincture with your favorite organic toothpaste!

SAGE TINCTURE

8 oz Universal Spirit
½ cup fresh sage gently crushed
(¼ cup dried sage)
8 oz water

Steep Universal Spirit and sage in an airtight container for 5 to 7 days. Taste test before straining and pressing solids to extract as much liquid as possible. After straining, dilute with water then bottle and store in a cool, dark place.

SAGE LIQUEUR

8 oz sage tincture
24 oz water, divided
1 cup sugar

In a small saucepan, combine 8 oz of the water over medium heat with the sugar just until the sugar dissolves. Remove from the heat and let cool. Blend the sage tincture, sugar solution, and remaining water. Bottle and seal in an airtight container – ready immediately!

SAGE BITTERS

4 oz sage tincture
4 oz bitters base (p 25)
8 oz water

Combine the sage tincture with the bitters base in a clean jar, then dilute with 8 oz water.

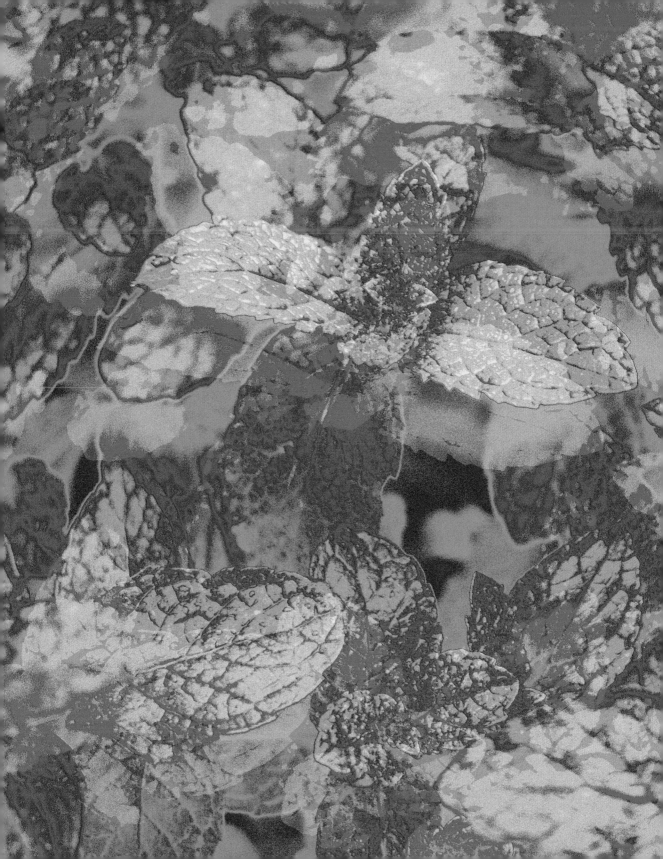

PEPPERMINT

Mentha x piperita

THE NAME OF THE genus *Mentha* comes from Greek mythology — the nymph Minthe was turned into the plant by Persephone, whose husband Hades was Minthe's lover. As a plant, she was trod upon and crushed, but was nonetheless admired for her delightful scent.

A cross between watermint and spearmint, peppermint is a fast-growing plant often used to flavor candies, desserts, alcoholic beverages, and even toothpaste for its cooling, refreshing flavor and aroma. Try variations on the below recipes with spearmint, which can be added to drinks like mint juleps and iced tea.

PEPPERMINT TINCTURE

8 oz Universal Spirit
½ cup fresh peppermint leaves
(¼ cup dried peppermint)
8 oz water

Steep Universal Spirit and peppermint in an airtight container for 5 to 7 days. Taste test before straining and pressing solids to extract as much liquid as possible. After straining, dilute with water then bottle and store in a cool, dark place.

PEPPERMINT LIQUEUR

8 oz peppermint tincture
24 oz water, divided
1 cup sugar

In a small saucepan, combine 8 ounces of the water over medium heat with the sugar just until the sugar dissolves. Remove from the heat and let cool. Blend the peppermint tincture, sugar solution, and remaining water. Bottle and seal in an airtight container – ready immediately!

PEPPERMINT BITTERS

4 oz peppermint tincture
4 oz bitters base (p 25)
8 oz water

Combine the peppermint tincture with the bitters base in a clean jar, then dilute with 8 ounces water.

CINNAMON

Cinnamomum cassia / Cinnamomum verum

CINNAMON IS AN AROMATIC spice derived from the inner bark of trees in the *Cinnamomum* family, the most common commercial species being *Cinnamomum cassia*. Highly prized in ancient times, it was often a gift for kings and gods, and was a coveted resource sought by explorers like Ferdinand Magellan throughout the 16th, 17th, and 18th centuries. Now widely available, cinnamon is used in a variety of sweet and savory dishes. It is often paired with chocolate in Mexico, combined with sugar and for baked goods and cereal in the United States, and is an important spice in both Turkish and Persian cuisine.

Try mixing this cinnamon tincture with your favorite chai tea to support digestion and reduce occasional stomach cramping.

CINNAMON TINCTURE

8 oz Universal Spirit
½ cup fresh cinnamon sticks, gently crushed
8 oz water

Steep Universal Spirit and cinnamon in an airtight container for 5 to 7 days. Taste test before straining and pressing solids to extract as much liquid as possible. After straining, dilute with water then bottle and store in a cool, dark place.

CINNAMON LIQUEUR

8 oz cinnamon tincture
24 oz water, divided
1 cup sugar

In a small saucepan, combine 8 ounces of the water over medium heat with the sugar just until the sugar dissolves. Remove from the heat and let cool. Blend the cinnamon tincture, sugar solution, and remaining water. Bottle and seal in an airtight container – ready immediately!

CINNAMON BITTERS

4 oz cinnamon tincture
4 oz bitters base (p 25)
8 oz water

Combine the cinnamon tincture with the bitters base in a clean jar, then dilute with 8 ounces water.

LAVENDER

Lavandula angustifolia

LAVENDER IS AN OLD-WORLD herb, cultivated for use in a variety of cuisines as well as for its essential oil — and of course, to add its namesake color to garden landscapes. The essential oil derived from the plant has many medicinal uses, being both antiseptic and anti-inflammatory. In aromatherapy, lavender is used for its calming and sleep-inducing properties. Dried buds of lavender are used in both sweet and savory cooking, often substituted for rosemary in the latter and in a variety of baked goods, sorbets, and desserts in the former.

Place a drop of your lavender tincture under your nose to awaken its stress relieving benefits through aromatherapy, or mix with water and sprinkle over your bed to promote a restful night's sleep.

LAVENDER TINCTURE

8 oz Universal Spirit
½ cup fresh lavender, gently crushed (¼ cup dried lavender)
8 oz water

Steep Universal Spirit and lavender in an airtight container for 5 to 7 days. Taste test before straining and pressing solids to extract as much liquid as possible. After straining, dilute with water then bottle and store in a cool, dark place.

LAVENDER LIQUEUR

8 oz lavender tincture
24 oz water, divided
1 cup sugar

In a small saucepan, combine 8 ounces of the water over medium heat with the sugar just until the sugar dissolves. Remove from the heat and let cool. Blend the lavender tincture, sugar solution, and remaining water. Bottle and seal in an airtight container – ready immediately!

LAVENDER BITTERS

4 oz lavender tincture
4 oz bitters base (p 25)
8 oz water

Combine the lavender tincture with the bitters base in a clean jar, then dilute with 8 ounces water.

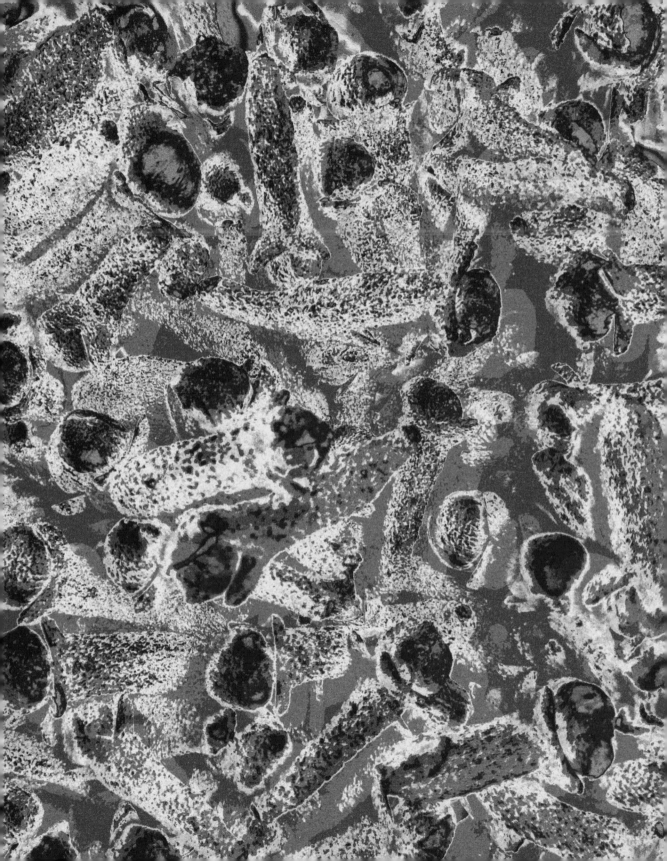

CLOVE

Syzygium aromaticum

CLOVES ARE AROMATIC FLOWER buds grown on the evergreen clove tree, native to Indonesia. Culinary uses include flavoring meats, curries, and marinades in Asian and Middle Eastern countries, and adding aromatic spice to warm beverages like the hot toddy. In Mexico, cloves are commonly paired with cumin and cinnamon. Cloves have also been smoked as cigarettes, and clove essential oil is often used in Indian and Chinese medicine as a toothache cure.

During the Renaissance, a ball filled with perfumes was worn to protect the wearer from plague or infection. A modern version of this perfumed container can be made by studding an orange with cloves (often in a decorative pattern) and letting it dry, creating a pleasant-smelling decoration.

CLOVE TINCTURE

8 oz Universal Spirit
½ cup fresh cloves, gently
  toasted and crushed
8 oz water

Steep Universal Spirit and cloves in an airtight container for 5 to 7 days. Taste test before straining and pressing solids to extract as much liquid as possible. After straining, dilute with water then bottle and store in a cool, dark place.

CLOVE LIQUEUR

8 oz clove tincture
24 oz water, divided
1 cup sugar

In a small saucepan, combine 8 ounces of the water over medium heat with the sugar just until the sugar dissolves. Remove from the heat and let cool. Blend the clove tincture, sugar solution, and remaining water. Bottle and seal in an airtight container – ready immediately!

CLOVE BITTERS

4 oz clove tincture
4 oz bitters base (p 25)
8 oz water

Combine the clove tincture with the bitters base in a clean jar, then dilute with 8 ounces water.

CHAMOMILE

Matricaria chamomilla, Chamaemelum nobile

CHAMOMILE IS A PERENNIAL plant native to Europe and North America, identifiable by its small white daisy-like flowers. Most often, Chamomile is consumed as an herbal tea, said to settle the stomach and aid sleep. It is also popular in aromatherapy for these same attributes. Its name comes from the Greek meaning "earth-apple," due to its apple-like scent.

CHAMOMILE TINCTURE

8 oz Universal Spirit
½ cup fresh chamomile flowers
   (¼ cup dried chamomile)
8 oz water

Steep Universal Spirit and chamomile in an airtight container for 5 to 7 days. Taste test before straining and pressing solids to extract as much liquid as possible. After straining, dilute with water then bottle and store in a cool, dark place.

CHAMOMILE LIQUEUR

8 oz chamomile tincture
24 oz water, divided
1 cup sugar

In a small saucepan, combine 8 ounces of the water over medium heat with the sugar just until the sugar dissolves. Remove from the heat and let cool. Blend the chamomile tincture, sugar solution, and remaining water. Bottle and seal in an airtight container – ready immediately!

CHAMOMILE BITTERS

4 oz chamomile tincture
4 oz bitters base (p 25)
8 oz water

Combine the chamomile tincture with the bitters base in a clean jar, then dilute with 8 ounces water.

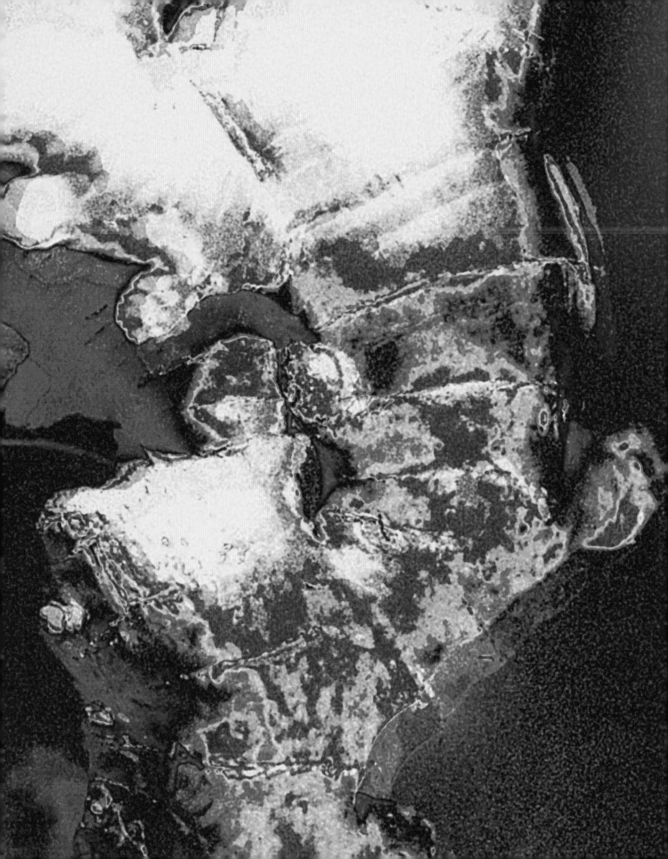

GINGER

Zingiber officinale

G INGER ROOT IS IN the same family *(Zingiberacaea)* as turmeric and cardamom. With roots in Southeast Asia, the spice was exported widely, with evidence of it being used by the Ancient Greeks and Romans, and arriving in Europe via the spice trade. It has many uses, both culinary and medicinal — from pickled ginger, ginger tea, and candied ginger to curries and kimchi. Traditionally, despite its spicy flavor, ginger is known to be soothing. It is effective against nausea, and has antioxidant and anti-inflammatory properties.

GINGER TINCTURE

8 oz Universal Spirit
½ cup fresh ginger root,
*   peeled and diced*
*   (¼ cup dried ginger)*
8 oz water

Steep Universal Spirit and ginger in an airtight container for 5 to 7 days. Taste test before straining and pressing solids to extract as much liquid as possible. After straining, dilute with water then bottle and store in a cool, dark place.

GINGER LIQUEUR

8 oz ginger tincture
24 oz water, divided
1 cup sugar

In a small saucepan, combine 8 ounces of the water over medium heat with the sugar just until the sugar dissolves. Remove from the heat and let cool. Blend the ginger tincture, sugar solution, and remaining water. Bottle and seal in an airtight container – ready immediately!

GINGER BITTERS

4 oz ginger tincture
4 oz bitters base (p 25)
8 oz water

Combine the ginger tincture with the bitters base in a clean jar, then dilute with 8 ounces water.

THYME

Thymus vulgaris

THYME IS A VERSATILE herb with a variety of uses. It is common in many cuisines, and is a component of both French herbs de Provence and the Middle Eastern za'atar spice blend. Dried thyme retains flavor remarkably well, making it a reliable kitchen staple. On the medicinal side, thyme was historically used for its antiseptic properties. Ancient Roman emperors believed eating thyme before or during a meal would prevent poisoning.

Both ancient Greeks and the knights of the Middle Ages believed thyme was a source of courage. Add a drop of this tincure or bitters to your drink any time you need a boost in bravery.

THYME TINCTURE

8 oz Universal Spirit
½ cup fresh thyme sprigs, gently crushed (¼ cup dried thyme)
8 oz water

Steep Universal Spirit and thyme in an airtight container for 5 to 7 days. Taste test before straining and pressing solids to extract as much liquid as possible. After straining, dilute with water then bottle and store in a cool, dark place.

THYME LIQUEUR

8 oz thyme tincture
24 oz water, divided
1 cup sugar

In a small saucepan, combine 8 ounces of the water over medium heat with the sugar just until the sugar dissolves. Remove from the heat and let cool. Blend the thyme tincture, sugar solution and remaining water. Bottle and seal in an airtight container – ready immediately!

THYME BITTERS

4 oz thyme tincture
4 oz bitters base (p 25)
8 oz water

Combine the thyme tincture with the bitters base in a clean jar, then dilute with 8 ounces water.

ROSEMARY

Rosmarinus officinalis

ROSEMARY IS A WOODY herb native to the Mediterranean. Its name, a combination of Latin words for "dew" and "sea," speaks to the way it thrives in coastal climates. The ancient Greeks, Romans, and Egyptians considered the plant sacred, offering healing powers and protection from evil spirits. Rosemary is also associated with remembrance — most memorably in Shakespeare's Hamlet, in a line delivered by Ophelia: "There's Rosemary, that's for remembrance, pray you love, remember." Ancient Greek students would wear rosemary in their hair, tie a garland around their necks, or even sleep with it under their pillow to improve their memory for exams.

ROSEMARY TINCTURE

8 oz Universal Spirit
½ cup fresh rosemary, gently crushed (¼ cup dried)
8 oz water

Steep Universal Spirit and rosemary in an airtight container for 5 to 7 days. Taste test before straining and pressing solids to extract as much liquid as possible. After straining, dilute with water then bottle and store in a cool, dark place.

ROSEMARY LIQUEUR

8 oz rosemary tincture
24 oz water, divided
1 cup sugar

In a small saucepan, combine 8 ounces of the water over medium heat with the sugar just until the sugar dissolves. Remove from the heat and let cool. Blend the rosemary tincture, sugar solution, and remaining water. Bottle and seal in an airtight container – ready immediately!

ROSEMARY BITTERS

4 oz rosemary tincture
4 oz bitters base (p 25)
8 oz water

Combine the rosemary tincture with the bitters base in a clean jar, then dilute with 8 ounces water.

LEMON

Citrus limon

ONE OF THE MOST common citrus fruits, the lemon is native to South Asia but has been cultivated for centuries across the Middle East, Mediterranean, and Europe. Widely used in both food and beverages, lemons also have cleansing properties — both around the house and within body and soul. Along with oranges and limes, lemons were historically consumed to prevent scurvy, which results from a deficiency in vitamin C. The below recipes can be adapted to any citrus fruit, or a blend of favorite varieties. When peeling fruit, make sure to avoid including any of the white pith, which will impart bitter flavors.

LEMON TINCTURE

8 oz Universal Spirit
½ cup lemon peel
8 oz water

Steep Universal Spirit and lemon peel in an airtight container for 5 to 7 days. Taste test before straining and pressing solids to extract as much liquid as possible. After straining, dilute with water then bottle and store in a cool, dark place.

LEMON LIQUEUR

8 oz lemon tincture
24 oz water, divided
1 cup sugar

In a small saucepan, combine 8 ounces of the water over medium heat with the sugar just until the sugar dissolves. Remove from the heat and let cool. Blend the lemon tincture, sugar solution, and remaining water. Bottle and seal in an airtight container – ready immediately!

LEMON BITTERS

4 oz lemon tincture
4 oz bitters base (p 25)
8 oz water

Combine the lemon tincture with the bitters base in a clean jar, then dilute with 8 ounces water.

HOLY BASIL

Ocimum tenuiflorum

HOLY BASIL IS AN herb native to Southeast Asia, with spiritual, medicinal, and culinary uses. The plant is sacred in the Hindu religion — where it is known as Tulsi — and is part of rituals worshipping Vishnu. Hindus often grow the plant in the courtyards of their houses, in special pots, or in plots adjacent to temples. Tulsi is often taken as an herbal tea in Ayurveda, a system of traditional medicine.

Holy basil tinctures can be combined with oils such as coconut or jojoba to treat eczema or relieve the itch of insect bites.

HOLY BASIL TINCTURE

8 oz Universal Spirit
½ cup fresh holy basil gently crushed (¼ cup dried basil)
8 oz water

Steep Universal Spirit and holy basil in an airtight container for 5 to 7 days. Taste test before straining and pressing solids to extract as much liquid as possible. After straining, dilute with water then bottle and store in a cool, dark place.

HOLY BASIL LIQUEUR

8 oz holy basil tincture
24 oz water, divided
1 cup sugar

In a small saucepan, combine 8 ounces of the water over medium heat with the sugar just until the sugar dissolves. Remove from the heat and let cool. Blend the holy basil tincture, sugar solution, and remaining water. Bottle and seal in an airtight container – ready immediately!

HOLY BASIL BITTERS

4 oz holy basil tincture
4 oz bitters base (p 25)
8 oz water

Combine the holy basil tincture with the bitters base in a clean jar, then dilute with 8 ounces water.

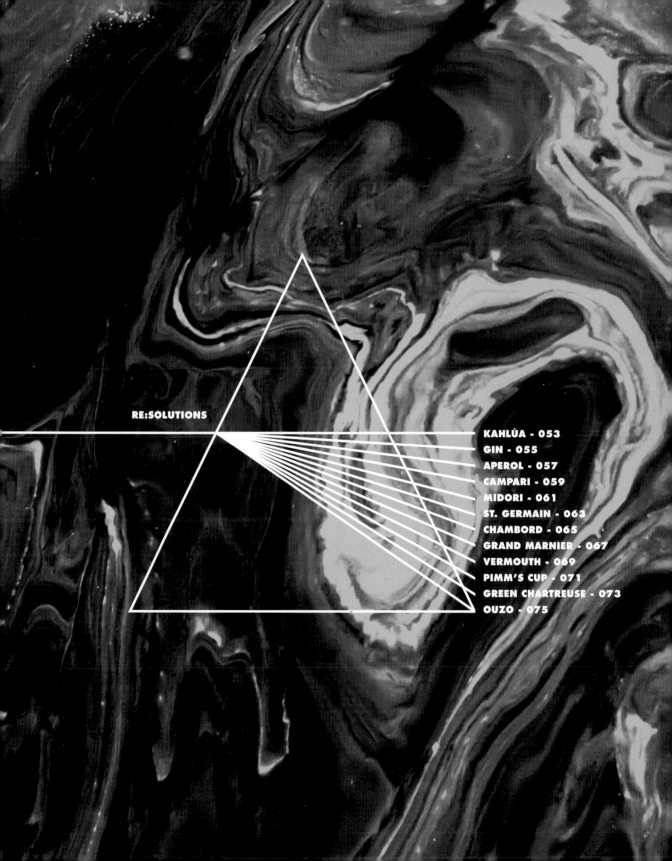

RE:SOLUTIONS

CHAPTER THREE

RE:SOLUTIONS

"Imitation is the sincerest form of flattery."

—Charles Caleb Colton

Beyond basic distilled spirits like whiskey and vodka, infused liqueurs have long been part of the cocktail scene. What most people don't know are the mysterious traditions and ingredients behind vermouth, aperitifs, liqueurs, and cordials. This chapter breaks down these classic concoctions, with recipes for the reader to mimic their flavor profiles at home.

The first recorded liqueurs descended from herbal medicine, with one of the oldest dating to the 13th century. Frangelico and Chartreuse both originated in monasteries. Other liqueurs, such as Campari, grew out of old world family recipes. Gin is one of the more widely recognized examples of a commonly available infused liquor. Having been in existence since the Middle Ages, its earliest roots stem from herbal medicine. Believed to preserve and suspend the potent health benefits found in herbs, medicinal spirits were one of the earliest pharmaceutical options in ancient times of sickness.

Alcoholic liquids have, unsurprisingly, also been used in tandem with religious rituals over the centuries. Passover Seder, the Eucharist, and Bacchanal are only a few ceremonies associated with a holy drink. The dual meaning of the word "spirit" within both religion and medicine is no small coincidence, as either use of the word offers a potential respite.

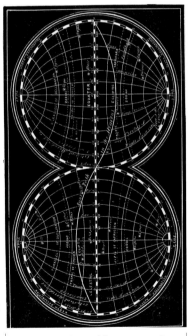

The growth, proliferation, and popularity of religion and spirits was followed by the industrial revolution and the advent of big business. Liqueurs once made in church cellars and basements were ushered into mass production, and recipes became standardized and commercialized. They could now be manufactured and distributed globally, for all to enjoy.

So why bother making your own, when you can so easily stroll to the market and buy a bottle? Because businesses had to make changes in order to offer consistent taste and to streamline production. Thus came the inclusion of artificial flavors, sweeteners, colors, and many more modern ingredients.

The following recipes will create 32 ounces, which is more than enough to fill a 750 ml bottle. Plan on there being approximately 6 ounces left to enjoy as a chef's treat, for your immediate enjoyment. Regardless, each recipe ensures that there will be enough to savor should you have plans to gift your full 750 ml bottle.

We have done our best to recreate the brand flavor and stay close to the proof of the original. Remember, since these are all natural, you may find that the liquids may seem thinner, appear cloudy, or contain some sediment. That is okay. Taste and flavor are our goals.

KAHLÚA

KAHLÚA IS THE MOST common coffee-flavored liqueur, and dates back to 1936 in Mexico. Containing rum, sugar, vanilla bean, and coffee, the 40 proof liqueur is used in common cocktails like the Espresso Martini and the White Russian, or consumed neat or over ice. Use in The Goat cocktail (p 127).

INGREDIENTS	INSTRUCTIONS

8 oz Universal Spirit
2 oz instant
    coffee crystals
1 vanilla bean,
    split and chopped
pinch of salt
24 oz water
2 cups light
    brown sugar
	Combine Universal Spirit, instant coffee, vanilla bean and salt in an airtight container and infuse in a cool, dark space for up to 1 week. Strain ingredients through a cheesecloth and dilute liquid with water before adding sugar and transferring to a clean container.

GIN

WHILE SOURCES VARY ON the exact time and location of
gin's origin, it dates back to at least the 17th-century in Europe — first
as an herbal remedy, then a commercialized spirit. Hundreds of flavors and
formulations of gin exist today — from the delicate rose and cucumber of
Hendrick's to classic Beefeater London Dry — with the only common theme
being the inclusion of juniper. The below recipe can be altered to your taste, by
adding more or less of each ingredient: more grapefruit, orange, or lemon for a
citrusy gin, more allspice and coriander for a spicier gin. Use this in The Bull
cocktail (p 111).

INGREDIENTS	INSTRUCTIONS
16 oz Universal Spirit	Combine Universal Spirit, juniper, coriander, allspice,
4 tbsps juniper	peppercorns, and cardamom in an airtight container
½ tsp coriander seeds	and infuse in a cool, dark space for up to 1 week.
7 allspice berries	Strain ingredients through cheesecloth and dilute
6 black peppercorns	liquid with water before transferring to a clean
5 cardamom pods	container. Add citrus ingredients and let sit 2 to 3
Peel of ¼ lemon	more days until preferred taste is reached.
Peel of ¼ grapefruit	
Peel of ¼ orange	
16 oz water	

APEROL

APEROL IS A CLASSIC Italian aperitif dating back to 1919. Similar in flavor to Campari, though a bit less bitter, it is commonly consumed in the Aperol Spritz cocktail. Use in The Ram cocktail (p 109), or make your own house spritz.

INGREDIENTS	INSTRUCTIONS
8 oz Universal Spirit ¼ cup orange zest 2 tbsps lemon zest 1 tbsp dried bitter orange peel 1 tbsp gentian root 1 tbsp cinchona 1 tsp cloves 1 tsp dried mint Pinch of salt 24 oz water 2 cups sugar	Combine Universal Spirit, orange zest, lemon zest, bitter orange peel, gentian root, cinchona, cloves, mint, and salt in an airtight container and infuse in a cool, dark space for up to 1 week. Strain ingredients through cheesecloth and dilute liquid with water before adding sugar and transferring to a clean container.

CAMPARI

ANOTHER POPULAR ITALIAN APERITIF, Campari dates back to 1860 and is an essential ingredient in several classic cocktails. Stronger and more bitter than Aperol, the liqueur is made from a proprietary recipe of herbs and fruit, and has a characteristic red color originally derived from crushed cochineal beetles. Using the recipe below as a guide, you can create your own version of the liqueur to add a distinctive touch to your Negroni, Americano, or spritz.

INGREDIENTS	INSTRUCTIONS
16 oz Universal Spirit *½ cup bitter orange peel* *2 tbsps lemon peel* *1 tbsp angelica root* *1 tbsp anise* *1 tbsp calamus* *1 tbsp fennel* *1 tbsp orris root* *1 tbsp wormwood leaves* *½ tbsp cloves* *1 tsp marjoram* *1 tsp sage* *1 tsp thyme* *1 tsp rosemary* *1 tsp cinnamon sticks* *½ cup plus ½ cup water* *½ cup plus ½ cup sugar* *1 tbsp hibiscus flower*	Combine Universal Spirit, bitter orange peel, lemon peel, angelica root, anise, calamus, fennel, orris root, wormwood, cloves, marjoram, sage, thyme, rosemary, and cinnamon in an airtight container and infuse in a cool, dark space for up to 1 week. Strain ingredients through a cheesecloth and dilute liquid with ½ cup water before adding ½ cup sugar. With the additional ½ cups of water and sugar, create a hibiscus simple syrup by combining ingredients with 1 tablespoon fresh hibiscus flower in a small saucepan over medium heat. After letting syrup steep for 30 minutes, combine with mixtures and transfer to a clean airtight container.

MIDORI

MIDORI IS THE JAPANESE word for "green," which makes sense after just one look at the almost-neon color of the liquid. The extremely sweet, muskmelon-flavored liqueur was introduced in the late 1970s, at a Studio 54 release party for the movie *Saturday Night Fever* — hence its disco vibes. This recipe uses fresh cantaloupe, honeydew, or any other favorite melon for a more natural flavor that plays well in modern cocktails. Try it in the First Born (p 113), Second Born (p 113), or The Fish (p 131) cocktails.

INGREDIENTS	INSTRUCTIONS
8 oz Universal Spirit *1 cup diced and muddled* *ripe cantaloupe or* *honeydew* *24 oz water* *2 cups sugar*	Combine Universal Spirit and melon in an airtight container and infuse in a cool, dark space for up to 1 week. Strain ingredients through cheesecloth and press melon to remove all excess liquid. Dilute remaining liquid with water before adding sugar and transferring to a clean container.

ST. GERMAIN

ST. GERMAIN IS AN elderflower liqueur considered by many to be a modern classic, introduced in 2007. Its delicate, sweet, floral flavor complements most white spirits, and can also be mixed with dry and/or sparkling wines in apértif-style drinks. Use in The Virgin (p 119).

INGREDIENTS	INSTRUCTIONS
8 oz Universal Spirit ¼ cup dried elderflower 1½ tsps lemon zest ¼ tsp salt 16 oz water, divided 8 oz honey	Combine Universal Spirit, elderflower, lemon zest, and salt in an airtight container and infuse in a cool, dark space for up to 1 week. Strain ingredients through cheesecloth and dilute liquid with 8 ounces water. Combine the remaining 8 ounces water with 8 ounces honey in a small saucepan over medium heat until combined and mix into the solution before storing in a clean container.

CHAMBORD

CHAMBORD IS A FRENCH raspberry liqueur. The brand was founded in 1982, but the recipe is inspired by one supposedly consumed by Louis XIV during a visit to the Château de Chambord. Its unique spherical bottle is modeled on a Globus cruciger, or "orb and cross," a medieval symbol of Christ's dominion over the world.

INGREDIENTS	INSTRUCTIONS
8 oz Universal Spirit *2 cups muddled* *raspberries* *24 oz water* *2 cups sugar*	Combine Universal Spirit and raspberries in an airtight container and infuse in a cool, dark space for up to 1 week. Strain ingredients through a cheesecloth and press berries to remove all excess liquid. Dilute remaining liquid with water before adding sugar and transferring to a clean container.

GRAND MARNIER, COINTREAU, ETC.

GRAND MARNIER AND COINTREAU are French brands introduced in the late 19th century, both of which are versions of the orange liqueur known as triple sec or curaçao. Cointreau is similar to a classic triple sec, which is a drier recipe. Dutch-style curaçao is sweeter, and shares a brandy base in common with Grand Marnier. Try the latter in The Virgin (p 199).

INGREDIENTS	INSTRUCTIONS
8 oz Universal Spirit ¼ cup orange zest 2 tbsps lemon zest 1 tbsp dried bitter orange peel Pinch of salt 24 oz water 2 cups sugar	Combine Universal Spirit, orange zest, lemon zest, bitter orange peel, and salt in an airtight container and infuse in a cool, dark space for up to 1 week. Strain ingredients through cheesecloth and dilute liquid with water before adding sugar and transferring to a clean container.

VERMOUTH

VERMOUTH IS AN AROMATIZED, fortified wine, first created for medicinal purposes. Later, it became popular as an aperitif, as well as a key ingredient in many classic cocktails. The Martini, the Manhattan, and the Negroni all require vermouth, and their popularity made it a staple of every good bar.

Vermouth gets its name from one of its traditional ingredients: wormwood, or *vermut* in German. This recipe includes wormwood alongside gentian root, another bittering agent, as well as some common kitchen herbs and warm spices for a moderately sweet, general herbal vermouth. Add more or less sugar to adjust the level of sweetness, or add/omit ingredients to create your ideal vermouth. Use in The Bull (p 111) and The Archer (p 125) cocktails.

INGREDIENTS	INSTRUCTIONS
4 oz Universal Spirit	Infuse all ingredients, including sugar, in an airtight
1 750 ml bottle	container for up to 1 week. Strain ingredients through
dry white wine	cheesecloth and dilute with water as necessary to
1 tsp wormwood	achieve desired sweetness level before storing in a
½ tsp gentian root	clean container.
½ tsp chamomile	
1 tbsp orange zest	
¼ tsp dried rosemary	
¼ tsp dried sage	
¼ tsp dried thyme	
4 toasted and crushed	
whole cloves	
1 toasted and crushed	
star anise	
¼ tsp grated nutmeg	
1 bay leaf	
1 cup sugar	

PIMM'S CUP

PIMM'S NO. 1 CUP is a traditionally English liqueur, first produced in 1823 by the owner of an oyster bar in the City of London. This first "tonic" was gin-based, contained a variety of herbs and botanicals, and was sipped as a kind of digestif. Years later, other versions (No. 2 Cup, No. 3 Cup, etc.) were introduced using different base spirits, though most are now phased out. Today, Pimm's Cup is combined with English-style carbonated lemonade and tons of chopped fruit for garnish, for a quintessentially English cocktail served at Wimbledon, Polo matches, and summer garden parties. Use in The Lion (p 177) and The Water Bearer (p 129) cocktails.

INGREDIENTS	INSTRUCTIONS
8 oz Universal Spirit	Infuse Universal Spirit, juniper berries, coriander
2 tbsps juniper berries	seeds, allspice, peppercorns, cardamom, bitter
½ tsps coriander seeds	orange peel, and orange zest and allow to steep for
7 allspice berries	up to 1 week. After infusing and straining, combine
6 black peppercorns	mixture with water, vermouth, and sugar.
5 cardamom pods	
1 tsps dried	
* bitter orange peel*	
Zest of 1 orange	
8 oz water	
16 oz vermouth (p 69)	
1 cup sugar	

GREEN CHARTREUSE

THE RECIPE FOR GREEN Chartreuse was set forth in a 1605 manuscript, and has been produced by Carthusian monks since 1737. The full recipe of 130 herbs, plants, and flowers is only known to the two monks who produce the liqueur. Named for the Grand Chartreuse monastery where the monks reside, the spirit's famous vibrant color actually gave its name to the color chartreuse, beginning in 1884. Its unique flavor profile — very sweet, yet still vegetal, herbaceous, and spicy — adds richness and complexity to classic cocktails like The Last Word. Also used in the First Born and Second Born cocktails (p 113)

INGREDIENTS	INSTRUCTIONS
8 oz Universal Spirit *4 oz of finely chopped fresh green herbs* *(3 oz if using dry)*	Steep Univeral Spirit and fresh green herbs for up to 2 days (fresh herbs can turn bitter fast, if using dry, test after 1 week). After infusing, strain herbs and reserve liquid.
1½ tsp lemon zest *1½ tsp orange zest* *3 star anise* *1 tsp whole coriander seed* *7 whole cloves* *24 oz water* *Honey to taste*	After creating base infusion, add lemon zest, orange zest, anise, coriander, and cloves and infuse for another week. After second infusion, strain ingredients add water and honey to taste, based on preferred sweetness level before transferring to a clean container. Suggested green herbs: *mint, tarragon, basil, dill, holy basil, thyme, parsley, lemon balm, lemon verbena, bay leaf, savory, lemongrass, scented geranium leaves, angelica, fennel fronds*

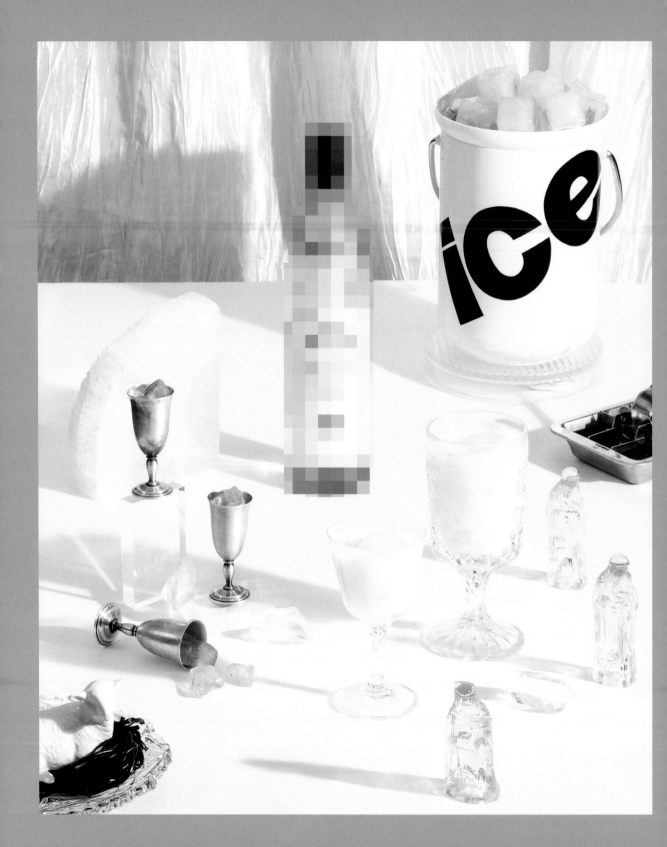

OUZO

OUZO IS AN ANISE-FLAVORED aperitif that originated in Greece, gaining popularity around the early 19th century. It is typically consumed as a shot (often chilled), or mixed with water (which turns it from clear to cloudy white) and sipped over ice. Beyond the anise which gives it its primary flavor, different distilleries use different combinations of spices like star anise, fennel, cardamom, and cloves to produce their signature recipe. The below recipe is a standard version, to which you are encouraged to add your own secret ingredients. Try it in The Crab cocktail (p 115).

INGREDIENTS	INSTRUCTIONS
16 oz Universal Spirit *10 star anise pods* *1 tsp licorice root* *1 tsp fennel seeds* *¼ tsp whole* *coriander seeds* *½ tsp anise seeds* *Pinch of salt* *16 oz water* *2 cups sugar*	Lightly toast star anise, licorice root, fennel seeds, coriander seeds, and anise in a pan over medium heat for 3 to 5 minutes, until a shade darker. Combine Universal Spirit, with toasted spices and salt in an airtight container and infuse in a cool, dark space for up to 1 week. Strain ingredients through cheesecloth and dilute liquid with water before adding sugar and transferring to a clean container.

INTENTIONAL SOLUTIONS

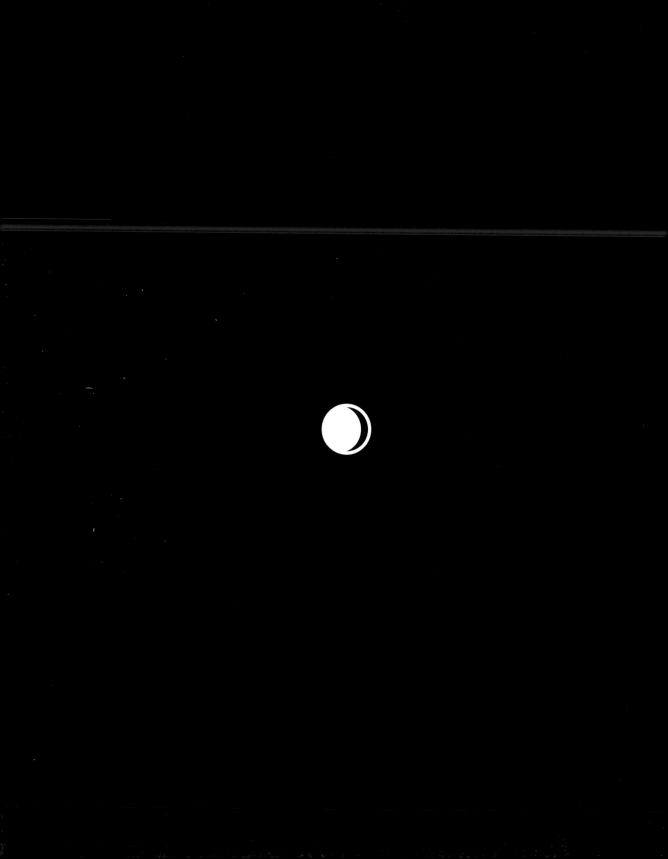

CHAPTER FOUR
INTENTIONAL SOLUTIONS

"Todo saldrá en la colada. / All will come out in the washing."
—Miguel de Cervantes

This chapter explores how to prepare cleansing tisanes and formulas with The Universal Spirit, to help you infuse your home, surroundings, and body with beneficial energy.

Since the universe is a creation of the mind, and every mind has the ability to think freely, we are in control of our universe. We are not only in control of what we create, we are, in effect, responsible for its maintenance (or lack thereof).

Cleaning on the physical plane is a concrete way to bring order to chaos. The energetic frequency in a space can be profoundly changed by uncluttering and tending to one's surroundings.

For example, imagine the sound an acoustic guitar might make with pebbles or a sponge inside. The process of removing unwanted and undesired items affects and changes the frequency with which a space resonates. The same is true of your home, body and life.

In the same way you might use a tuner to bring a guitar into harmony, the following formulas are designed to help you and your surroundings get "in tune." For your home we have a spray and for your body temple there is a tisane for ingestion.

The process of spiritual and energetic cleaning is also an expression of love. The physical and metaphysical worlds each have direct influence upon each other and are holistically entwined. For example, keeping a clear mind helps to maintain a clean home, and keeping a clean home can help maintain a clear mind. These principles can also be applied to what you imbibe, as well as the contents of the products you use to clean your space.

To garner the most ideal outcomes, we encourage you to concoct a solution that matches the vibrational frequency you desire. For easy reference, dear reader, the solutions in this chapter are organized by intention. Feeling lonely? Look to Aphrodite's Juju for more passionate date nights. Need help with a decision? Let the Wisdom of King Solomon guide your mind.

The recipes for Physical Cleaning Solutions listed in the pages that follow are meant to be used in your physical space — your home, possessions, and other surroundings. Use as a surface cleanser or room spray to affect the cosmic balance of your environment in your favor.

The Metaphysical Cleaning Solutions are meant to be ingested — a solution for the temple of your body. In order to achieve your desired vibrational frequency, add a few drops of the solution to your tea, water, or other beverage.

LOVE / APHRODITE'S JUJU / VENUS

PHYSICAL CLEANING SOLUTION

INGREDIENTS	INSTRUCTIONS

2 oz Universal Spirit
6 oz water
3 drops coriander
   essential oil
5 drops spearmint
   essential oil
7 drops orange
   essential oil
9 drops rose
   essential oil
	In a clean spray bottle add all ingredients, cover, and shake to combine. Shake well prior to each use.

METAPHYSICAL CLEANING SOLUTION

INGREDIENTS	INSTRUCTIONS

4 oz Universal Spirit
1 tsp coriander seeds
1 tsp dried spearmint
1 tsp dried
   orange peel
1 tbsp dried
   rose petals
4 oz water
	In a clean 8-ounce jar with an airtight lid, add the Universal Spirit and all the dried herbs. Seal the jar, give it a good shake, and store in a cool, dark place for one week. Be sure to shake and focus your intention into the jar daily.
	
	After one week, dilute a drop of the tincture with an equal drop of water and taste. If the flavor is to your liking, proceed to strain. If not, reseal the jar and continue to steep for up to another week while continuing to shake and taste daily.
	
	Strain the mixture through a fine mesh sieve or small colander lined with cheesecloth or a clean tea towel into a clean, small bowl or other container. Press on the soaked herbs to extract as much liquid as possible.
	
	Dilute the liquid with equal parts water (about 4 ounces) and transfer to a small dropper bottle. To use this tincture, place 5 to 10 drops into 8 ounces of water, tea, or any beverage of your choosing.

PEACE / JOY / LOVE OF THE DOVE

PHYSICAL CLEANING SOLUTION

INGREDIENTS	INSTRUCTIONS
2 oz Universal Spirit 6 oz water 8 drops chamomile essential oil 8 drops lavender essential oil 8 drops rosemary essential oil	In a clean spray bottle add all ingredients. Cover and shake to combine. Shake well prior to each use.

METAPHYSICAL CLEANING SOLUTION

INGREDIENTS	INSTRUCTIONS
4 oz Universal Spirit 2 tsps dried chamomile 2 tsps dried rosemary (or 4 tsps fresh) 4 oz water	In a clean 8-ounce jar with an airtight lid, add the Universal Spirit and all the dried herbs. Seal the jar, give it a good shake and store in a cool, dark place for one week. Be sure to shake, and focus your intention into the jar daily. After one week, dilute a drop of the tincture with an equal drop of water and taste. If the flavor is to your liking, proceed to strain. If not, reseal the jar and continue to steep for up to another week while continuing to shake and taste daily. Strain the mixture through a fine mesh sieve or small colander lined with cheesecloth or a clean tea towel into a clean, small bowl or other container. Press on the soaked herbs to extract as much liquid as possible. Dilute the liquid with equal parts water (about 4 ounce) and transfer to a small dropper bottle. To use this tincture, place 5 to 10 drops into 8 ounces of water, tea, or any beverage of your choosing.

EQUITY / LADY JUSTICE / COURT CASE / FAIR PLAY

PHYSICAL CLEANING SOLUTION

INGREDIENTS	INSTRUCTIONS
2 oz Universal Spirit 6 oz water 8 drops licorice essential oil 8 drops allspice essential oil 8 drops fennel essential oil	In a clean spray bottle add all ingredients. Cover and shake to combine. Shake well prior to each use.

METAPHYSICAL CLEANING SOLUTION

INGREDIENTS	INSTRUCTIONS
4 oz Universal Spirit 2 tsps allspice berries, crushed 2 tsps licorice root chips 2 tsps fennel seeds, crushed 4 oz water	In a clean 8-ounce jar with an airtight lid, add the Universal Spirit and all the dried herbs. Seal the jar, give it a good shake, and store in a cool, dark place for one week. Be sure to shake and focus your intention into the jar daily. After one week, dilute a drop of the tincture with an equal drop of water and taste. If the flavor is to your liking, proceed to strain. If not, reseal the jar and continue to steep for up to another week while continuing to shake and taste daily. Strain the mixture through a fine mesh sieve or small colander lined with cheesecloth or a clean tea towel into a clean, small bowl or other container. Press on the soaked herbs to extract as much liquid as possible. Dilute the liquid with equal parts water (about 4 ounces) and transfer to a small dropper bottle. To use this tincture, place 5 to 10 drops into 8 ounces of water, tea, or any beverage of your choosing.

SEX / MAGICK D'EROS / HOT HOODOO

PHYSICAL CLEANING SOLUTION

INGREDIENTS	INSTRUCTIONS
2 oz Universal Spirit 6 oz water 9 drops of cinnamon essential oil 15 drops of jasmine essential oil	In a clean spray bottle add all ingredients. Cover and shake to combine. Shake well prior to each use.

METAPHYSICAL CLEANING SOLUTION

INGREDIENTS	INSTRUCTIONS
4 oz Universal Spirit 1½ tsps cinnamon, coarsely ground 1½ tbsps jasmine tea 4 oz water	In a clean 8-ounce jar with an airtight lid, add the Universal Spirit and all the dried herbs. Seal the jar, give it a good shake, and store in a cool, dark place for one week. Be sure to shake and focus your intention into the jar daily. After one week, dilute a drop of the tincture with an equal drop of water and taste. If the flavor is to your liking, proceed to strain. If not, reseal the jar and continue to steep for up to another week while continuing to shake and taste daily. Strain the mixture through a fine mesh sieve or small colander lined with cheesecloth or a clean tea towel into a clean, small bowl or other container. Press on the soaked herbs to extract as much liquid as possible. Dilute the liquid with equal parts water (about 4 ounces) and transfer to a small dropper bottle. To use this tincture, place 5 to 10 drops into 8 ounces of water, tea, or any beverage of your choosing.

GOOD LUCK / ANTI-JINX / LADY LUCK / FORTUNA

PHYSICAL CLEANING SOLUTION

INGREDIENTS	INSTRUCTIONS
2 oz Universal Spirit *6 oz water* *8 drops chamomile essential oil* *8 drops clove essential oil* *8 drops lemon verbena essential oil*	In a clean spray bottle add all ingredients. Cover and shake to combine. Shake well prior to each use.

METAPHYSICAL CLEANING SOLUTION

INGREDIENTS	INSTRUCTIONS
4 oz Universal Spirit *2 tsps chamomile* *2 tsps whole cloves, crushed* *2 tsps dried lemon verbena* *4 oz water*	In a clean 8-ounce jar with an airtight lid, add the Universal Spirit and all the dried herbs. Seal the jar, give it a good shake, and store in a cool, dark place for one week. Be sure to shake and focus your intention into the jar daily. After one week, dilute a drop of the tincture with an equal drop of water and taste. If the flavor is to your liking, proceed to strain. If not, reseal the jar and continue to steep for up to another week while continuing to shake and taste daily. Strain the mixture through a fine mesh sieve or small colander lined with cheesecloth or a clean tea towel into a clean, small bowl or other container. Press on the soaked herbs to extract as much liquid as possible. Dilute the liquid with equal parts water (about 4 ounces) and transfer to a small dropper bottle. To use this tincture, place 5 to 10 drops into 8 ounces of water, tea, or any beverage of your choosing.

SUCCESS / ABUNDANCE / PROSPERITY / PLENITUDE

PHYSICAL CLEANING SOLUTION

INGREDIENTS	INSTRUCTIONS
2 oz Universal Spirit *6 oz water* *6 drops peppermint* *essential oil* *6 drops ginger* *essential oil* *12 drops chamomile* *essential oil*	In a clean spray bottle add all ingredients. Cover and shake to combine. Shake well prior to each use.

METAPHYSICAL CLEANING SOLUTION

INGREDIENTS	INSTRUCTIONS
4 oz Universal Spirit *1½ tsps dried* *peppermint* *1½ tsps ginger,* *freshly peeled* *and grated* *1 tbsp dried chamomile* *4 oz water*	In a clean 8-ounce jar with an airtight lid, add the Universal Spirit and all the dried herbs. Seal the jar, give it a good shake and store in a cool, dark place for one week. Be sure to shake, and focus your intention into the jar daily. After one week, dilute a drop of the tincture with an equal drop of water and taste. If the flavor is to your liking, proceed to strain. If not, reseal the jar and continue to steep for up to another week while continuing to shake and taste daily. Strain the mixture through a fine mesh sieve or small colander lined with cheesecloth or a clean tea towel into a clean, small bowl or other container. Press on the soaked herbs to extract as much liquid as possible. Dilute the liquid with equal parts water (about 4 ounces) and transfer to a small dropper bottle. To use this tincture, place 5 to 10 drops into 8 ounces of water, tea, or any beverage of your choosing.

FORTUNE & WEALTH / TENDER LOVE / MONEY STAY WITH ME

PHYSICAL CLEANING SOLUTION

INGREDIENTS	INSTRUCTIONS

2 oz Universal Spirit
6 oz water
6 drops orange
  essential oil
6 drops chamomile
  essential oil
6 drops clove
  essential oil
6 drops ginger
  essential oil
	In a clean spray bottle add all ingredients. Cover and shake to combine. Shake well prior to each use.

METAPHYSICAL CLEANING SOLUTION

INGREDIENTS	INSTRUCTIONS

4 oz Universal Spirit
1½ tsp dried
  orange peel
1½ tsp
  dried chamomile
1½ tsp dried
  cloves, crushed
1½ tsp ginger,
  fresh grated
4 oz water
	In a clean 8-ounce jar with an airtight lid, add the Universal Spirit and all the dried herbs. Seal the jar, give it a good shake, and store in a cool, dark place for one week. Be sure to shake and focus your intention into the jar daily.
	
	    After one week, dilute a drop of the tincture with an equal drop of water and taste. If the flavor is to your liking, proceed to strain. If not, reseal the jar and continue to steep for up to another week while continuing to shake and taste daily.
	
	    Strain the mixture through a fine mesh sieve or small colander lined with cheesecloth or a clean tea towel into a clean, small bowl or other container. Press on the soaked herbs to extract as much liquid as possible.
	
	    Dilute the liquid with equal parts water (about 4 ounces) and transfer to a small dropper bottle. To use this tincture, place 5 to 10 drops into 8 ounces of water, tea, or any beverage of your choosing.

BLESSINGS / HAPPY FAMILY / ANCESTRAL CLEARING

PHYSICAL CLEANING SOLUTION

INGREDIENTS	INSTRUCTIONS

2 oz Universal Spirit
6 oz water
8 drops basil
   essential oil
8 drops lavender
   essential oil
8 drops marjoram
   essential oil
	In a clean spray bottle add all ingredients. Cover and shake to combine. Shake well prior to each use.

METAPHYSICAL CLEANING SOLUTION

INGREDIENTS	INSTRUCTIONS
4 oz Universal Spirit 2 tsps dried basil 2 tsps dried lavender 2 tsps dried marjoram 4 oz water	In a clean 8-ounce jar with an airtight lid, add the Universal Spirit and all the dried herbs. Seal the jar, give it a good shake, and store in a cool, dark place for one week. Be sure to shake, and focus your intention into the jar daily. After one week, dilute a drop of the tincture with an equal drop of water and taste. If the flavor is to your liking, proceed to strain. If not, reseal the jar and continue to steep for up to another week while continuing to shake and taste daily. Strain the mixture through a fine mesh sieve or small colander lined with cheesecloth or a clean tea towel into a clean, small bowl or other container. Press on the soaked herbs to extract as much liquid as possible. Dilute the liquid with equal parts water (about 4 ounces) and transfer to a small dropper bottle. To use this tincture, place 5 to 10 drops into 8 ounces of water, tea, or any beverage of your choosing.

STRENGTH / PILLARS OF HERCULES / COURAGE

PHYSICAL CLEANING SOLUTION

INGREDIENTS	INSTRUCTIONS
2 oz Universal spirit 6 oz water 4 drops essential oil 8 drops allspice essential oil 12 drops thyme essential oil	In a clean spray bottle add all ingredients. Cover and shake to combine. Shake well prior to each use.

METAPHYSICAL CLEANING SOLUTION

INGREDIENTS	INSTRUCTIONS
4 oz Universal Spirit 1 tsp whole black peppercorns, crushed 2 tsps whole allspice, crushed 1 tbsp dried thyme 4 oz water	In a clean 8-ounce jar with an airtight lid, add the Universal Spirit and all the dried herbs. Seal the jar, give it a good shake, and store in a cool, dark place for one week. Be sure to shake and focus your intention into the jar daily. After one week, dilute a drop of the tincture with an equal drop of water and taste. If the flavor is to your liking, proceed to strain. If not, reseal the jar and continue to steep for up to another week while continuing to shake and taste daily. Strain the mixture through a fine mesh sieve or small colander lined with cheesecloth or a clean tea towel into a clean, small bowl or other container. Press on the soaked herbs to extract as much liquid as possible. Dilute the liquid with equal parts water (about 4 ounces) and transfer to a small dropper bottle. To use this tincture, place 5 to 10 drops into 8 ounces of water, tea, or any beverage of your choosing.

ENERGY /
TOWER
OF POWER /
VITALITY

PHYSICAL CLEANING SOLUTION

INGREDIENTS	INSTRUCTIONS

2 oz Universal spirit
6 oz water
12 drops orange
  essential oil
12 drops lemon
  essential oil
	In a clean spray bottle add all ingredients. Cover and shake to combine. Shake well prior to each use.

METAPHYSICAL CLEANING SOLUTION

INGREDIENTS	INSTRUCTIONS
4 oz Universal Spirit 1 tbsp fresh orange zest 1 tbsp fresh lemon zest 4 oz water	In a clean 8-ounce jar with an airtight lid, add the Universal Spirit and all the dried herbs. Seal the jar, give it a good shake, and store in a cool, dark place for one week. Be sure to shake and focus your intention into the jar daily. After one week, dilute a drop of the tincture with an equal drop of water and taste. If the flavor is to your liking, proceed to strain. If not, reseal the jar and continue to steep for up to another week while continuing to shake and taste daily. Strain the mixture through a fine mesh sieve or small colander lined with cheesecloth or a clean tea towel into a clean, small bowl or other container. Press on the soaked herbs to extract as much liquid as possible. Dilute the liquid with equal parts water (about 4 ounces) and transfer to a small dropper bottle. To use this tincture, place 5 to 10 drops into 8 ounces of water, tea, or any beverage of your choosing.

AWAKENING / WISDOM OF KING SOLOMON / EPIPHANY

PHYSICAL CLEANING SOLUTION

INGREDIENTS	INSTRUCTIONS
2 oz Universal Spirit 6 oz water 11 drops lime essential oil 13 drops sage essential oil	In a clean spray bottle add all ingredients. Cover and shake to combine. Shake well prior to each use.

METAPHYSICAL CLEANING SOLUTION

INGREDIENTS	INSTRUCTIONS
4 oz Universal Spirit 1 tbsp lime zest 1 tbsp dried sage 4 oz water	In a clean 8-ounce jar with an airtight lid, add the Universal Spirit and all the dried herbs. Seal the jar, give it a good shake, and store in a cool, dark place for one week. Be sure to shake and focus your intention into the jar daily. After one week, dilute a drop of the tincture with an equal drop of water and taste. If the flavor is to your liking, proceed to strain. If not, reseal the jar and continue to steep for up to another week while continuing to shake and taste daily. Strain the mixture through a fine mesh sieve or small colander lined with cheesecloth or a clean tea towel into a clean, small bowl or other container. Press on the soaked herbs to extract as much liquid as possible. Dilute the liquid with equal parts water (about 4 ounces) and transfer to a small dropper bottle. To use this tincture, place 5 to 10 drops into 8 ounces of water, tea, or any beverage of your choosing.

CLARITY/ PURIFICATION / DEVIL BE GONE / SANCTIFICATION

PHYSICAL CLEANING SOLUTION

INGREDIENTS	INSTRUCTIONS
2 oz Universal Spirit *6 oz water* *8 drops nutmeg essential oil* *8 drops pine essential oil* *8 drops lemon verbena essential oil*	In a clean spray bottle add all ingredients. Cover and shake to combine. Shake well prior to each use.

METAPHYSICAL CLEANING SOLUTION

INGREDIENTS	INSTRUCTIONS
4 oz Universal Spirit *1 tsp pine needles, crushed* *1 tsp nutmeg, freshly grated* *2 tbsps dried lemon verbena* *4 oz water*	In a clean 8-ounce jar with an airtight lid, add the Universal Spirit and all the dried herbs. Seal the jar, give it a good shake, and store in a cool, dark place for one week. Be sure to shake and focus your intention into the jar daily. After one week, dilute a drop of the tincture with an equal drop of water and taste. If the flavor is to your liking, proceed to strain. If not, reseal the jar and continue to steep for up to another 7 days while continuing to shake and taste daily. Strain the mixture through a fine mesh sieve or small colander lined with cheesecloth or a clean tea towel into a clean, small bowl or other container. Press on the soaked herbs to extract as much liquid as possible. Dilute the liquid with equal parts water (about 4 ounces) and transfer to a small dropper bottle. To use this tincture, place 5 to 10 drops into 8 ounces of water, tea, or any beverage of your choosing.

COSMIC SOLUTIONS

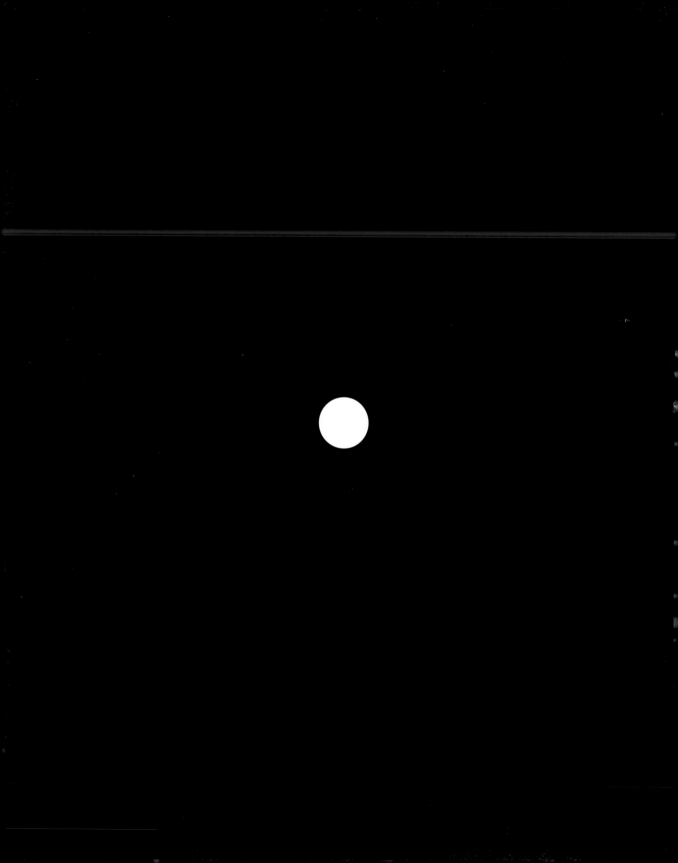

CHAPTER FIVE

COSMIC SOLUTIONS

"The stars above us govern our conditions."

—*William Shakespeare*

This chapter is based around astrological signs and solutions. The term zodiac, which is derived from a Greek word meaning "circle of animals," refers to both the area of the sky adjacent to the path of the Sun, as well as the twelve "signs" that correspond to constellations within this area. This division originated in Babylonian culture, and carried through to the Greeks and Romans. A Hindu system, while based on different stellar coordinates, has many of the same symbols — for example, the Hindu "water-pitcher" corresponds to the Greek Aquarius, or "water-carrier."

The Chinese zodiac is also divided into twelve signs, but these are not associated with constellations, and cycles through years rather than months. It corresponds with the lunar calendar, invented by the first Chinese emperor, Huangdi, in 2637 BC. According to legend, the order of animals was determined by a great race, where the first 12 animals to cross a river would make up the zodiac.

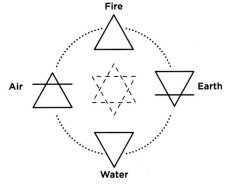

The signs used in Western astrology are divided into four groups:

Fire Signs: Aries, Sagittarius, Leo	Air Signs: Libra, Aquarius, Gemini
Water Signs: Cancer, Scorpio, Pisces	Earth Signs: Capricorn, Taurus, Virgo

In all of these cases, a person's sign — based on the date of their birth — has been used to predict or reflect characteristics of personality across many cultures.

The division of these signs relates not only to one's personality, but also life events such as relationships, finances, and travel. The following pages include cocktails based around the herbs and botanicals best suited for your astrological sign to promote health, happiness, and inner well-being. Based on each sign's characteristics, each drink's ingredients were chosen to play up your sign's strengths and combat its weaknesses.

ARIES

MARCH 21 APRIL 19

THE RAM

2 oz Aperol (p 57)
1 oz pressed valencia
    orange juice
½ oz pressed blood orange juice
3 dashes cinnamon tincture (p 31)
Orange peel expression
Ground cayenne rim

Wet the rim of a coupe glass with
an orange wedge before dipping
in ground cayenne, shaking off any
excess. Combine all ingredients in a
shaker with ice and shake vigorously
before pouring into rimmed glass.
Express an orange peel over the top
of the drink.

Strengths	*Weaknesses*
Courageous, determined, confident, enthusiastic, optimistic, honest, passionate	*Impatient, moody, short-tempered, impulsive, aggressive*

ARIES IS A VERY hot-tempered sign. People born under this sign are predisposed to such illnesses as headaches, sinusitis, neuralgia, and eye problems. Because Aries is a fire sign ruled by the planet Mars, plants associated with this element and planet usually have thorns or prickles. They are also spicy or bitter in flavor or are red in color. Aries rules the head, eyes, and face, so the best plants for Aries are those that purify the blood, stimulate the adrenal glands, or are high in iron because of Mars' ruling over the mineral iron. The astrologers advise Aries to use thyme, angelica, lemon balm, mint, and valerian root for relieving headaches and relaxing the body. Barberry, rosehip, aloe vera, juniper, and stinging nettle are good blood cleaners and a source of a great deal of vitamins.

TAURUS

APRIL 20 MAY 20

THE BULL

3 oz gin (p 55)
½ oz vermouth (p 69)
¼ oz pomegranate juice
3 dashes thyme tincture (p 41)
Rose water mist
Dandelion leaf

Stir gin, vermouth, pomegranate juice, and thyme tincture in a chilled glass filled with ice for 30 seconds before straining and transferring to a martini glass. Mist with rose water and garnish with a dandelion leaf before serving.

Strengths	*Weaknesses*
Reliable, patient, practical, devoted, responsible, stable	*Stubborn, possessive, uncompromising*

TAURUS IS AN EARTH sign ruled by the planet Venus. Venus is the planet that represents desire and beauty, so Taurus plants often have gorgeous flowers and enticing fragrances. Tauruses are food lovers, which is probably why people born under this sign often have problems with digestion, metabolic disorders, and neck, throat, and trachea diseases. Because Taurus rules the throat and ears, the best plants for the Bull are often soothing to the throat, or may calm the digestive system after overindulging in the finest foods. Tauruses should use rosemary, anise, and marjoram for the digestive system; Saint John's wort and pine buds for colds; and thyme, mint and marsh-mallow as sedative and anti-bacterial remedies.

GEMINI

MAY 21 JUNE 20

FIRST BORN

2 oz Chartreuse (p 73)
1 oz Midori (p 61)
½ oz pressed lemon juice
3 dashes lavender tincture (p 33)
Lavender sprig

Combine Chartreuse, Midori, Meyer lemon, and lavender tincture in a chilled glass filled with ice and stir for 30 seconds before straining into a coupe glass. Garnish with a lavender sprig before serving.

SECOND BORN

1 oz Chartreuse (p 73)
½ oz Midori (p 61)
3 dashes lavender tincture (p 33)
Splash of lemonade
Lavender sprig

Build all ingredients in a Collins glass over ice, beginning with Chartreuse and finishing with splash of lemonade. Garnish with a lavender sprig before serving.

Strengths	*Weaknesses*
Gentle, affectionate, curious, adaptable, ability to learn quickly and exchange ideas	*Nervous, inconsistent, indecisive*

RULED BY THE PLANET Mercury, Gemini is an air sign that governs the lungs, shoulders, arms, and hands. It is the most worrisome sign of the zodiac, and tends to cause a weak nervous system. Such people are prone to skin and nervous system diseases, bronchitis, lung illnesses, acute respiratory infections, neuralgia of clavicle-shoulder girdle. Gemini's plants usually feature finely divided leaves or stems (like the bronchi of lungs), hairy or fuzzy leaves (related to the cilia in the lungs), or subtle odors. Plants associated with Gemini help to strengthen the lungs and respiratory system, or relax the nervous system. The best herbs for Gemini include eucalyptus leaves, chamomile, elecampane, licorice, hawthorn, Saint John's wort, red clover, vervain, comfrey, parsley, dill, caraway, fennel, carrot, and valerian.

CANCER

JUNE 21 JULY 22

THE CRAB

1½ oz Universal Spirit
1 oz water
1 oz pressed white
grapefruit juice
½ oz ouzo (p 75)
3 dashes rosemary tincture (p 43)
Rosemary sprig

Stir Universal Spirit, water, grapefruit juice, and ouzo in a chilled glass with ice. Strain and pour into a rocks glass with one large ice cube, then garnish with 3 dashes of rosemary tincture and a rosemary sprig.

Strengths	*Weaknesses*
Tenacious, highly imaginative, loyal, emotional, sympathetic, persuasive	*Moody, pessimistic, suspicious, manipulative, insecure*

BECAUSE CANCER IS A water sign and is ruled by the moon, Cancer's plants generally have soft or moon-shaped leaves, contain a lot of moisture, or are found near water. Oftentimes they are white in color, or have white or pale yellow flowers. Cancer rules the stomach, breasts, diaphragm, and liver, so plants that aid digestion or affect the subconscious are associated with the sign of the Crab. St. John's wort and stinging nettle leaves can help to relieve stomach pain. Pumpkin, corn silk, dandelion and immortelle can be used to treat gallbladder inflammation. The most beneficial herbs for Cancer are linden, elderflowers, saxifrage, sage, rosemary, and purslane.

LEO

JULY 23 AUGUST 22

THE LION

2 oz Pimm's Cup (p 71)
1 oz Canton ginger liqueur
1 oz pressed tangerine juice
½ oz pressed lemon juice
4 dashes turmeric tincture
Lemon peel

Build Pimm's, Canton Ginger Liqueur, tangerine juice, lemon juice, and turmeric tincture in a Collins glass over ice. Garnish with a lemon peel before serving.

Strengths	*Weaknesses*
Creative, passionate, generous, warm-hearted, cheerful, humorous	*Arrogant, stubborn, self-centered, lazy, inflexible*

NATURALLY, LEO IS A fire sign ruled by the brilliant sun. The part of the body ruled by Leo the Lion is the heart, which predisposes Leos to having vulnerable cardiovascular systems. They often acquire such maladies as ischemia, angina, back and chest pain, neurosis, and gallbladder diseases. Leo's plants are usually large and gold or orange in color, or have heart-shaped leaves or a radiating shape. Plants that regulate blood pressure and have an uplifting effect on the spirit are most beneficial to Leo. Herbs for Leo are represented by coltsfoot, burdock, chamomile, linden blossom, anise, angelica, calendula, elecampane, mint, dandelion, fennel, dill, and parsley.

VIRGO

AUGUST 23
SEPTEMBER 22

THE VIRGIN

Strengths	Weaknesses
Loyal, analytical, kind, hardworking, practical	*Shyness, worry, overly critical of self and others, all work and no play*

1½ oz St. Germain (p 63)
½ oz Grand Marnier (p 67)
3 dashes sage tincture (p 27)
Splash of champagne
Edible flower garnish

Shake St. Germain, Grand Marnier, and sage tincture in a shaker with ice. Pour into a rocks glass over ice before topping with champagne and garnishing with edible flowers.

VIRGO IS AN EARTH sign ruled by the planet Mercury. Virgo is traditionally the Goddess of the Grain, and is associated with autumn. Her plants often have finely divided leaves or stems, subtle odors, or small, brightly-colored flowers. The most beneficial plants for Virgo are high in potassium and help to calm the nerves. Virgo's most wide-spread illnesses are digestive disorders and colitis. People born under the Virgo sign should utilize the following medicinal herbs and products: blueberries, strawberries, lavender, mint, sage, lemon verbena, rosemary, savory, valerian, Saint John's wort, centaury.

LIBRA

SEPTEMBER 23 OCTOBER 22

THE SCALES

2 oz Granny Smith apple
simplest solution (p 17)
½ oz Canton ginger liqueur
Splash of apple cider vinegar
2 dashes cinnamon tincture (p 31)
2 dashes nutmeg tincture
Splash of hard cider
Dried apple

Stir Apple Liqueur, Canton Ginger Liqueur, apple cider vinegar, cinnamon tincture, and nutmeg tincture in a glass with ice. Strain and pour into a martini glass before topping with a splash of hard cider and garnishing with a dried apple slice.

Strengths	*Weaknesses*
Cooperative, diplomatic, gracious, fair-minded, social	*Indecisive, avoids confrontations, will carry a grudge, self-pity*

LIBRA IS AN AIR sign, and is ruled by the planet Venus. Because Venus is the planet of beauty and love, Libra's plants often have light, lovely flowers and gorgeous scents. Libra rules the kidneys and the adrenals, so her plants help to bring balance to these areas of the body. Libras are said to have good health, but some diseases may occur such as hypertension, headaches, kidney and urinary tract illnesses, metabolic disorders. The recommended herbs are jasmine, mint, carnation, clover, oregano, rosemary, stinging nettle, tricolor viola, barberries, mallow, yarrow, sage, and coltsfoot.

SCORPIO

OCTOBER 23
NOVEMBER 21

THE SCORPION

1 oz Chambord (p 65)
2 oz dry Irish stout
½ oz anise liqueur
2 dashes black pepper tincture
1 blackberry, speared

Combine Chambord, dry Irish stout, and anise liqueur in a shaker with ice. Shake vigorously and pour into two shot glasses. Top with 2 dashes of black pepper tincture and speared blackberry before serving.

Strengths	*Weaknesses*
Passionate, driven, perceptive, emotional, sacrificing, determined	*Vindictive, paranoid, destructive, possessive, jealous, clingy*

A WATER SIGN RULED BY both Mars and Pluto, Scorpio's plants are often found in remote places or underground. They will likely have thorns, be red in color, and grow under adversity. The reproductive organs are ruled by Scorpio, so plants that balance the hormones, regulate the menstrual cycle, or help with childbirth and pregnancy are very beneficial to Scorpio. Because of their vulnerability to urogenital diseases, hepatitis, hemorrhoids, and venereal diseases, astrological science advises people born under this sign to use rosehip, honeysuckle, ginger, chamomile, shelf fungus, stinging nettle, wormwood, basil, mustard, wheatgrass, psyllium, coriander, and aloe vera.

SAGITTARIUS

NOVEMBER 22 DECEMBER 21

THE ARCHER

3 oz vermouth (p 69)
½ oz cranberry juice
3 dashes sage tincture (p 27)
3 cranberries, speared

Shake vermouth, cranberry juice, and sage tincture in a shaker with ice. Pour into a rocks glass and garnish with 3 speared cranberries.

Strengths	*Weaknesses*
Generous, idealistic, great sense of humor	*Promises more than can deliver, very impatient, will say anything no matter how undiplomatic*

SAGITTARIUS IS A FIRE sign that is ruled by the large and optimistic planet Jupiter. Therefore, the Archer's plants tend to be large in size and fairly conspicuous, with a pleasant odor. The best plants for Sagittarius will support the liver, are high in the mineral silica, and promote a positive frame of mind to combat this sign's tendency to suffer from rheumatism, sciatica, blood disorders, and liver diseases. Herbs for Sagittarius are burdock root, horsetail, juniper berries, borage, common betony, ash-tree root, stinging nettle, saffron, sage, and thyme.

CAPRICORN __

DECEMBER 19
JANUARY 19

THE GOAT

1 oz hazelnut liqueur
3 oz Kahlúa (p 53)
1 oz half-and-half
Cocoa powder

Combine hazelnut liqueur, Kahlúa, and half-and-half in a shaker with ice. Shake vigorously before straining into a rocks glass over ice. Garnish with a dusting of cocoa powder before serving.

Strengths	*Weaknesses*
Responsible, disciplined, self-control, good managers	*Know-it-all, unforgiving, condescending, expecting the worst*

CAPRICORN IS REGARDED AS an irritated and anxious sign. People born under the Capricorn sign are likely to have digestive system diseases, teeth and skin problems, liver illnesses, skeletal system and joint disorders, and colds. As an Earth sign ruled by the planet Saturn, Capricorn's plants usually have few flowers, are knobby or woody, and may have an unpleasant smell or taste. Saturn rules plants with long lives and slow growth, so plants with annual rings are also associated with the Goat. And because Capricorn rules the knees, joints, bones, and teeth, plants that are high in calcium can be very beneficial. They should try to use such herbs as ginseng, *Shisandra chinensis,* bilberries, blackcurrant, lemon balm, honeysuckle, cornflower, knotgrass, and needles of coniferous trees.

AQUARIUS

JANUARY 20 FEBRUARY 18

THE WATER BEARER

2 oz Pimm's Cup (p 71)
2 oz cold-pressed celery juice
½ oz pressed grapefruit juice
3 dashes chamomile tincture (p 37)
2 dashes fennel tincture
Mint sprig

Build Pimm's, cold-pressed celery juice, grapefruit juice, chamomile tincture, and fennel tincture in a Collins glass over ice. Garnish with a mint sprig and serve.

Strengths	*Weaknesses*
Progressive, original, independent, humanitarian	*Runs from emotional expression, temperamental, uncompromising, aloof*

AQUARIUS IS A SUPER-ACTIVE and nervous sign. Such people are inclined to blood and lymphatic system diseases, varicose veins, and nervous system disorders. Aquarius is an air sign ruled by odd-ball Uranus, so the Water-bearer's plants will grow in unusual places and may vary in appearance. The most healing and beneficial plants for Aquarius are ones that help circulation, relax the nervous system, or promote inspiration. The most useful herbs for them are wormwood, oregano, lemon balm, feijoa, capsella, ginseng, *Schisandra chinensis,* hawthorn, and yarrow.

PISCES

FEBRUARY 19
MARCH 20

THE FISH

2 oz Midori (p 61)
3 oz dry white wine
Splash of seltzer
4 dashes violet tincture

Combine Midori and dry white wine in a chilled glass with ice. Strain and pour into a Collins glass over ice before adding a splash of seltzer and 4 dashes of violet tincture.

Strengths	*Weaknesses*
Compassionate, artistic, intuitive, gentle, wise, musical	*Fearful, overly trusting, sad, desire to escape reality, can be a victim or a martyr*

PISCES IS A WATER sign ruled by Jupiter and Neptune. This deeply sensitive and charming sign is known for its idealism, dramatic tendencies, and natural dumb luck. This sensitivity translates to Pisces' health as well, making them exceptionally vulnerable to colds, sinus trouble, and water retention within the body. Pisces should try useful green tea with jasmine and chamomile flowers in order to improve mood and relieve fatigue. Their medicinal plants include cowberry leaves, sage, mint, mulberry, calendula, wild strawberries, wild chicory, chestnut, burdock, daisy, anise, and chamomile.

CONVERSION CHARTS

Metric and Imperial Conversions

(These conversions are rounded for convenience)

Ingredient	Cups/ Tablespoons/ Teaspoons	Ounces	Grams/ Milliliters
Fruit, dried	1 cup	4 ounces	120 grams
Fruits or veggies, chopped	1 cup	5 to 7 ounces	145 to 200 grams
Fruits or veggies, puréed	1 cup	8.5 ounces	245 grams
Honey, maple syrup, or corn syrup	1 tablespoon	0.75 ounce	20 grams
Liquids: cream, milk, water, or juice	1 cup	8 fluid ounces	240 milliliters
Salt	1 teaspoon	0.2 ounces	6 grams
Spices: cinnamon, cloves, ginger, or nutmeg (ground)	1 teaspoon	0.2 ounce	5 milliliters
Sugar, brown, firmly packed	1 cup	7 ounces	200 grams
Sugar, white	1 cup/ 1 tablespoon	7 ounces/0.5 ounce	200 grams/12.5 grams
Vanilla extract	1 teaspoon	0.2 ounce	4 grams

Liquids

8 fluid ounces = 1 cup = ½ pint
16 fluid ounces = 2 cups = 1 pint
32 fluid ounces = 4 cups = 1 quart
128 fluid ounces = 16 cups = 1 gallon

ACKNOWLEDGMENTS

Steve, Rona & Kate
Mom & Dad
Kreider & Silas
The Grasses
Kwei Fong Hao
The Cromptons
The Kirks
The Mecholskys
The Lees
Myself
All those that take it over the Finish Line
Everyone at QCM & Gyro
Everyone who makes me laugh
Gage Johnston
Pink Pasdar
Pamela Raju
Bethe Hayes
Olive Ledlie
Nathanial Hornblower
Anthony Williams
Jane & John Bennett
Michael, Antoinette & Amanda Alan
Brian Alan & Laura

Potucek
Edward & Elizabeth Alan
Grandmom & Granddad
Nanny & Grandfather
Aunt Rose
Aunt Sherri
FAM: Aunt Mary
The Kurtz Family
The Szvetecz Family
John & Lizzie Lavender
Denise & Louis Cook
Rebecca Renio
Liz Jacoby
Maria Eife
Leigh & Ann Horowitz
Pearl, Annette & the McGlynns
Eva Yashinsky
Buddy
Max Vandenberg
Oskar Kalinowski
Lee Noble
Bre Furlong
Kelli Haugh
Caroline Mills

Wade Keller
John & Jennifer Newton
Bill Donahue
Kyle Richards
Howard Wills
Comicbookgirl19
Hermes Trismegistus
Thoth
Gaia
Spirit Science
Infinite Creator
Prince
Alan Moore
Stan Lee
RuPaul
The Galactic Federation of Light
St. Michael the Archangel
All Guardian Angels
The Pleiadians
Light Workers
The Italian Market
South Philadelphia
Beth Beverly

INSTANT SOLUTIONS: COCKTAILS

Cosmicpolitans
1 part Universal Spirit
½ parts GRAND MARNIER
2 parts Cranberry Juice
(unsweetened)
½ part Lime Juice
Shake over ice. Strain,
Serve with a TWIST ∞

MOSCOW MULE
1 part UNIVERSAL SPIRIT
2 parts Ginger Beer
½ part Lime Juice
Blend over ICE.

SEA BREEZE
1 part Universal Spirit
3 parts Cranberry Juice
(unsweetened)
1 part GRAPEFRUIT Juice
½ part LIME JUICE
Blend OVER ICE

↳ BAY BREEZE
Substitute Grapefruit
with Pineapple Juice

+ ⬜ X V

BLOODY MARY
1 PART UNIVERSAL
SPIRIT
4 PARTS BLOODY
MARY MIX
Blend over ICE —
Serve with celery OR
PICKLE SURPRISE

BEST BLOODY MARY MIX:
4 oz tomato juice
½ oz Lemon Juice
½ oz OLIVE or PICKLE
JUICE
2 DASHES TOBASCO
2 Dashes of SOY SAUCE
1 pinch Celery Salt
1 pinch Black Pepper
1 pinch Smoked
paprika
Mix it all together,
FAM!

PURPLE JESUS

1 part Universal Spirit
2 parts Ginger Ale
1 part GRAPE JUICE
Blend over Ice.

?HUNCH PUNCH?
-OR-
TRASHCAN PUNCH
-OR-
JUNGLE JUICE

1 part Universal Spirit
2 parts Lemonade
2 parts Orange Juice
2 parts FRUIT PUNCH
2 parts Lemon Lime Soda
        or Club Soda
In a tRash can oR other
LARGE, Clean Container
STIR IT ALL Up.
Serve with a Lot
        Of Ice.

SHOTS:

Lemondrops
1 part Universal Spirit
1 part LemonADE
1 part Lemon Juice
½ part Grand Marnier

KAMIKAZE
1 part Universal Spirit
1 part LemonADE
1 part Lime Juice
½ part Grand Marnier

Ch·Ch·Cherry BOMBS
1 part Universal Spirit
2 part ENERGY DRINK
Splash Grenadine

PINEAPPLE UPSIDE DOWN CAKE
1 part UNIVERSAL SPIRIT
2 parts Pineapple Juice
Splash if Grenadine

CHOCOLATE CAKE
1 part Universal Spirit
1 part Lemon Juice
2 part Hazelnut Liqueur

JELLO SHOTS:
3 oz package of Jello,
1 cup Boiling water, ¼ cup Universal Spirit.
3/4 cup COLD WAter. Dissolve in HOT, add COLD & U

DIRTY Martinis :
  2 parts UNIVERSAL SPIRIT
  1 part Vermouth
  $\frac{1}{2}$-1 part OLIVE JUICE
  1-2 parts Water → OLIVE Garnish

DIRTY GIBSONS:
  2 parts Universal SPIRIT
  1 part Vermouth
  $\frac{1}{2}$-1 parts Pickled Onion Juice
  1-2 parts Water → ONION Garnish

3 OLIVE Garnish
1. Health
2. Wealth
3. Happiness
∞

☉ = sun   ⊕ = earth
☽ = moon   ⊖ = salt

*FOR BOTH : Shake very well over ICE.
      Strain & Serve immediately
      (chill the glass)

GIMLETS
2 parts Universal
      SPIRIT
1 part Lime Juice
$\frac{1}{2}$-1 part Simple
      Syrup
1-2 parts Water

Shake over ICE.
Strain & Serve

SECTS on the BEACH
1 part Universal SPIRIT
$\frac{1}{2}$ parts Peach Schnapps
$\frac{1}{2}$ parts Cassis
2 parts CRANBERRY J.
2 parts PINEAPPLE J
1 part ORANGE J

Blend over ICE.

Ƴ Ƭ ᴟᴦ ᴟ ᴟ ᵮ Ʒ ƒ Ʋ Ʋ ᴍ Ʋ̄ ᴟᴍ
A B C D E F G H I J K L M

SANGRIA ... 4 WAYS

Basic Ratios:
1 part Universal SPIRIT
5 parts WINE
1 part CLUB soda
Chopped FRUIT

Blend all ingredients in a pitcher — CHILL for a couple hours before serving.

RED SANGRIA ♣

1 part Universal Spirit
5 parts RED Wine
(merlot, Cab Savv., Malbec)
1 part CLUB Soda
1 part tart CHERRY Juice
 (or Cranberry)
FRUIT: Cherries, Straw-
berries, Red Fruits

WHITE SANGRIA ◇

1 part UNIVERSAL Spirit
5 parts White WINE
(Savv. Blanc. Pinot Grig)
1 part CLUB Soda
1 part White Grape Juice
FRUIT: White peach,
peeled apples, pears,
 white sage

BLACK SANGRIA ♡

1 part UNIVERSAL Spirit
1 part RED WINE
(merlot, Cab.Savv, Malbec)
1 part CLUB Soda
1 part Cassis
FRUIT: Red grape,
Black Berries, plums

GOLD SANGRIA ♠

1 part UNIVERSAL SPIRIT
5 parts White Wine
(Sauvignon Blanc, Pinot
Grig, dry Riesling)
1 parts CLUB Soda
1 part GINGER Liqueur
FRUIT: Pineapple, Peach,
Oranges, Tangerines

N O P Q R S T U V W X Y Z

BLACK RUSSIANS

1 part UNIVERSAL SPIRIT
1 part Cola
1 part KahLua
Blend over ICE.
⭐ ⭐ ⭐ ⭐ ⭐

WOOB RUSSIANS

1 part UNIVERSAL SPIRIT
1 part Creme Soda
1 part KahLua
½ part Heavy C.R.E.A.M.
(or coconut cream)
Blend over ICE.

SCREWDRIVERS

1 part UNIVERSAL SPIRIT
3 parts ORANGE JUICE
Splash of Orange Blossom
water (if feeling fancy)
Blend over ICE.

11 A
        AB
        ABRA
        ABRAC
        ABRACA
        ABRACAD
        ABRACADA
        ABRACADAB
        ABRACADABR
        ABRACADABRA

For HARVEY WALL BANGERS: float a
shot of Galliano on top.
For GREYHOUNDS: Substitute Grapefruit
Juice for OJ (known as a "LAVENDER" in
some diner circles).

• MUDSLIDES •
1 part UNIVERSAL SPIRIT
1 part KahLua
1 part IRISH CReam
2 parts MILK or cream
8 parts ICE
BLEND It ALL UP.

WOO·WOO
1 part UNIVERSAL SPIRIT
½ part Peach Schnapps
2 parts CRANBERRY
½ parts LIME JUICE
Blend over ICE.

NOTES

NOTES

NOTES

NOTES

NOTES

NOTES

NOTES

NOTES

NOTES

INDEX

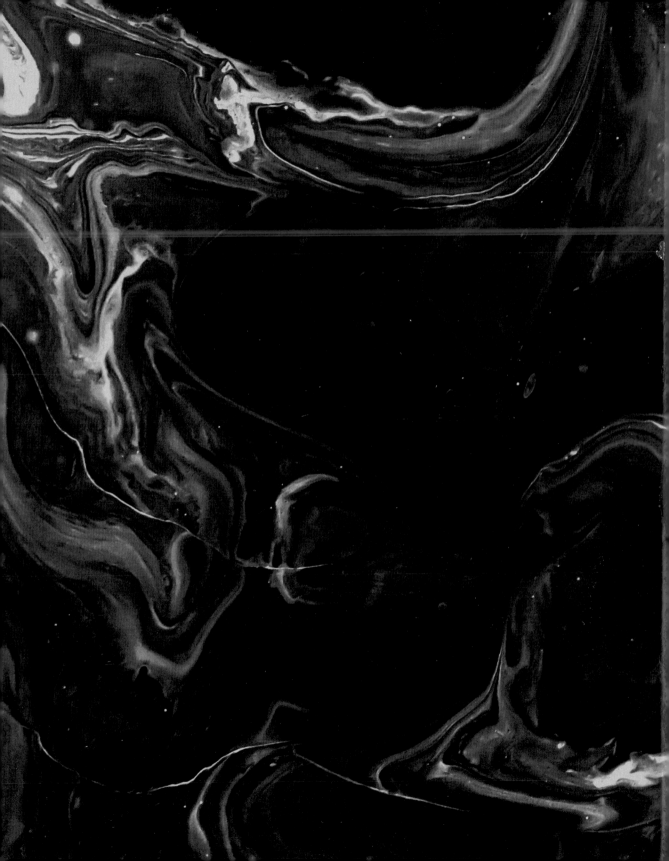